GUIDE TO CHRISTIAN LIVING: USING THE BIBLE IN YOUR DAILY LIFE

GUIDE TO CHRISTIAN LIVING: USING THE BIBLE IN YOUR DAILY LIFE

Written and compiled by
Rev. Otis Blue

To order additional copies of this book, contact:
Xlibris Corporation
1-888-795-4274
www.Xlibris.com
Orders@Xlibris.com
37437

CONTENTS

DEDICATION

I dedicate this work to my family, brothers and sisters, the congregation of my church, to my fellow clergy and to all mankind that seek to know and understand the Word of God and teachings of the Bible. I also acknowledge the contribution made by others to the research, compilation, and writing of this book which has been a major undertaking that involved others too numerous to mention here. Over the years, as I studied the Bible as part of my ministry and began the process of putting this book together, the advice, expertise and support of others proved to be pivotal. To these men and women, I express my sincere gratitude for their contribution that made it possible for me to complete the task of putting this book together. I am also thankful to all those that encouraged me on to this point: my brother, Rev. W. C. Blue and my pastor, Rev. Andrew Dowdell, Sr.

Foreword

Rev Otis Blue has a deep knowledge of the Bible, great insight into the philosophy of Christianity; and a profound understanding of the historical perspectives that form the Christian religion in addition to a total grasp of the Christian religion and the role it has played in shaping the world in which we live. The contents of this work bear testimony to that fact: that he has the depth and breadth of knowledge needed to undertake a work of such magnitude. The result is this book, which in many ways has no parallel, and does what no other book has done before. He has taken the great teachings of the Bible and broken them down to a level where anyone can understand.

This is a profound book in every sense of the word. It educates, informs and even entertains, all at once, and succeeds in doing so in a rather folksy style, making it easy to relate to

This is the kind of book that can be aptly described as an all-purpose book. For those seeking to understand the Bible, and to relate to its teachings in a realistic manner, it succeeds in doing just that. Not only does it cover almost all the books in the Bible; it discusses the main points of all the books focusing on such topics as who wrote it, when it was written, for what reason, its context in relation to other books of the Bible and in what circumstances, and most importantly, the meaning and significance of the great Biblical stories. You can't get this kind of knowledge from just reading the Bible.

For those lost souls seeking salvation, it easily converts into a prayer book of powerful lamentations that answer to various needs.

For those seeking counseling and guidance, it provides the kind of wise counseling and advice that are premised on the teachings of the Bible and which lead to more than happy lives on this earth: they lay the foundation for the godly life which leads to salvation.

Unassuming, even unpretentious, and low-key as he would be described in today's terms, Rev Blue has accomplished a great feat which puts him up there with men and women of the cloth who have distinguished themselves as outstanding scholars and brilliant writers in addition to the work they do on behalf of the church.

Nothing is lost in the process, which in itself a remarkable feat. Not the intellectual profundity of the ancient Biblical scholars whose wisdom, knowledge and writings were more mystical than they were mundane and couldn't be easily understood by the untutored.

It is quite evident that Rev Blue has high aspirations; as a minister, to take his ministry to another level, and to provide readers with a work that will contribute to their understanding of the Bible. That's why he spent years researching, writing, compiling and putting together this great book,

Does that make Rev Blue a Biblical scholar? Certainly, and in more ways than one. It shows he has a keen intellect that seeks answers to questions that can be found only in the Bible.

Reference for others who work in the ministry. This work easily fits into that category. While it may seem like a summary of some of the great teachings in the Bible, it also succeeds in presenting the reader with introductory readings that lead to more comprehensive readings on the subject in the Bible for those seeking more clarification or further elaboration.

It is not by any means perfect. The author and compiler makes no such claim. It has its strong points and its weaknesses and even its flaws. Those who might be tempted to view it as serious scholarly writing would be less than thrilled to find out that no attempt is made to create and or sustain a scholastic aura. Rather it is punctuated with flashes of brilliance, insight and wisdom, backed by the usual religious knowledge we all know only too well.

Make up Your Mind To Study God's Word

So many Christians skim over their Bibles haphazardly, thinking they are studying God's Word, and then they wonder why their "study time" is not producing any changes in their lives. A casual reading will not do. The truth is contained in God's Word. Once it takes hold in our heart, it brings change in our lives. We must seek out those truths. Spend time reading and pondering and mediating them. We must consider their impact on our lives, and prayerfully humble ourselves to change our lives when we need to in light of new revelation received.

This is the true study. When you read a verse or passage, ask yourself. *What does this mean to me? How does this affect My Life?* Never allow anyone else, such as your pastor, to do your studying for you. Always insist on doing it yourself.

For the Logos of God is a living thing, active and more cutting than any double-edged sword, penetrating to the very division of soul and spirit, joints and marrow, scrutinizing the very thoughts and conceptions of the heart. No created thing is hidden from Him; all things lie open and exposed before the eyes of Him with whom we have to reckon. (Hebrews 4:12, 13)

Be Systematic About Your Study

Do not just take up subjects at random. Think about what you would like to study and make a list. Then go down your list and take up the topics, one by one, and begin a thorough study. This will help you to avoid studying the same topic over and over.

Make Prayer an Important Part Of Study Preparation

As you prepare to study, you need to ask the Lord to reveal to you what He has for you that day. Every time you open your Bible, ask God to open your spiritual eyes for discernment. If you ask, He will reveal Himself to you through His Word every time.

Howbeit when he, the Spirit of truth is come, he will guide you into all truth: for he shall not speak of himself: but whatsoever he shall hear, that he shall speak: and he will show you things to come. He shall glorify me: for he shall receive of mine, and shall show unto you.

The Ephesians and Colossian prayers are excellent to pray with before studying the Bible. They are in the first person to make them easier to use.

"That the God of our Lord Jesus Christ, the Father glory, may give unto me the spirit of wisdom and revelation in the knowledge of You.

That eyes of me understanding are being enlightened; that I may know what is the hope of His inheritance in the saints, and what is the exceeding greatness of His mighty power.

Which You wrought in Christ, when You raised Him from the dead. And set Him at your right hand in the heavenly places, far above all principality, and power, and might, and dominion, and every name that is named, not only in the world, but also in that which is to come. And have put all things under His feet, and gave Him to be the Head over all things to the church, which is his body, the fullness of Him that fills all in all. (Ephesians 1:17-23)

That You would grant me, according to the riches of His glory, to be strengthened with the might by His sprit in my inner man; that Christ may dwell in my heart and faith; that I am being rooted and grounded in love. That I may be able to comprehend with all saints what is the breadth, and length, and depth, and height; and to know the love of Christ, of which passes knowledge, that I might be filled with all the fullness of God.

Now unto him that is able to do exceeding abundantly above all that I ask of things, according to the power that works in me, unto him be glory in the church by Christ Jesus throughout all ages, world without end. Amen (Ephesians 3:16-21)

For there cause I, since the day I heard the Gospel, do not cease to pray, and to desire that I might be filled with the knowledge of Your will in all spiritual wisdom and understanding; that I might walk the worthy of the Lord into all pleasing, being fruitful in every good work, and increasing in the knowledge of God; strengthened with all might, according to Your glorious power, unto all patience and longsuffering with joyfulness.

I give thanks unto the Father, Who has made me able to be a partaker of the inheritance of the saints in light: Who has delivered me from the power of darkness, and has translated me into the kingdom of His dear Son, the Son of love. In whom I have redemption through His blood, even the remission of sin (Colossians 1:9-14)

WAS JESUS GOD?

Matthew records one of the most challenging questions asked of anyone. It is, "What think ye of Christ? Whose son is he?" (Matthew 22:42.) What about his divinity? Was Jesus God? In his gospel, John builds an unanswerable argument designed to prove that Jesus of Nazareth is the divine Son of God. And he frankly declares that he wrote his book that his readers "might believe that Jesus is the Christ, the Son of God; and believing "they" might have life through his name." (John 20:31)

1. **Did Christ exist before coming to this world?**

    The first words in John's gospel reveal that God the Son is co-eternal with God the Father. "In the beginning was the word, and the Word was with God, and the Word was God. The same was in the beginning with God. All things were made by him; and without him was not any thing made that was made." John 1:1-13. That Word which took part in the creation of the world was Jesus (John 1:14)

    Jeremiah called the Messiah "THE LORD OUR RIGHTEOUS-NESS" (Jeremiah 23:5-6). The Hebrew *Yahweh* (Jehovah), "the self-existent One" is here applied to the Messiah. The text shows both His power and divine nature.

2. **Was Jesus divine or was He only man? How does God the Father refer to Him?**

    "But unto the Son he saith, Thy throne, O God, is for ever and ever; a sceptre of righteousness is the sceptre of thy kingdom. Thou hast loved righteousness, and hated iniquity: therefore God, even thy God hath anointed thee with the oil of gladness above thy fellows." (Hebrew 1:8, 9.)

3. **What did Jesus say about His existence before His birth in human flesh?**

    "And now, O Father, glorify thou with thine own self with the glory which I had with thee before the world was." (John 17:5)

Note: Take a look at Isaiah 9:6 where the prophet calls Christ the Father. Read about Him in the Baptist's testimony in John 1:15, 30 "He was before me" (though Jesus was born after John). Paul says, "He is before all things." Colossians 1:17. Then there is Christ's own witness in John 8:58 where He says, "Before Abraham was, I am." Read also Exodus 3:14. This name 'I am' both in the Hebrew and in the English is a form of the verb "to be" and implies that He is the eternal, self-existing One.

4. **Through what power was the incarnation of Jesus made possible?**
   "And the angel answered and said unto her, The Holy Ghost shall come upon thee, and the power of the Highest shall overshadow thee: therefore also that holy thing which shall be born of thee shall be called the Son of God." Luke 1:35

Note: The Father, Son, and Holy Sprit worked together in the act of incarnation. Incarnation has to do with Christ becoming man. The incarnation of Christ did not in any way annul His divinity. The Scripture says, "And without controversy, great is the mystery of godliness: God was manifest in the flesh, justified in the Spirit, seen of angels, preached unto the Gentiles, believe in the world, received up into glory." 1 st Timothy 3:16. When Christ was born the announcement of the angels to the shepherds referred to Him as the Saviour. Read Luke 2:11. Matthew 1:21-23 speaks of Him as "Emmanuel . . . God with us."

5. **What reason is given in Hebrew why Christ became man?**
   "Wherefore in all things it behoved him to be made like unto his brethren, that he might be a merciful and faithful high priest in things pertaining to God, to make reconciliation for the sins of the people." Hebrew 2:17

6. **How did the Father refer to Jesus?**
   "And lo a voice from heaven saying, This is my beloved Son, in whom I am well pleased." Matthew 3:17

7. **How did Jesus demonstrate He had the power of God, that He is the Son of God, and that He is God the Son?**

   a.   He had power to read human heart (John 2:24,25)
   b.   He had power to foretell the future (John 13:19)

    c.   He had creative power (John 6:1-20)

    d.   He had power to give life (John: 21)

    e.   He had infallibility of utterance (John 8:46)

    f.   He had power to forgive sins (Mark 2:1-12)

    g.   He had the right to receive worship (Matthew 14:33)

Note: This is an important point since created beings such as men and angels are not to be worshiped. Read Acts 10:25, 26; Revelations 22:8, 9; Matthew 4:8-10. But Jesus accepted worship of His disciples as Deity. Thomas said of Him, "My Lord and my God." John 20:28, 29 Angels also worship Him (Hebrews 1:6). Ultimately all the universe will adore Him (Philippians 2:10).

    h.   He had the power to raise the dead to life (John 5:25)

    i.   He had the power to transform hearts (John 1:12, 13).

Note: Only a divine being could truthfully say, "I am the light of the world"; "I am the resurrection, and the life"; "I am the door"; "I am the way, the truth, and the life."

8. **How could Christ be David's Lord as well as his Son?**

    The Pharisees had answered Christ's question, "Whose son is he [the Christ]?" by saying. "The son of David," Matthew 22:42. Then Jesus referred to Psalm 110:1 where David called the Messiah "Lord." This would indicate the Messiah was older than David. If this is so, then how could the Messiah be David's son and in this position be younger than David? The Jewish Leaders were unprepared to answer this question, "I David then call him Lord: how is he son?" Matthew 22:45. Had they faced this question properly, they would have had to admit Jesus to be the Messiah, the Son of God.

Conclusion

    The record of Matthew indicated that Jesus was born of a virgin (Matthew 1:18, 22-25). Paul declares, "But when the fullness of the time was come, God sent forth his Son, made of a woman, man under the law, to redeem then that were under the law, that we might receive the adoption of sons." (Galatians 4:4-5.) He is referred to as "holy, harmless, undefiled, separate from sinners." (Hebrews 7:26.)

Concerning His relationship to the Father, Paul says, "In him dwelleth all the fullness of the Godhead bodily." Colossians 2:9.

We cannot help but acknowledge as did the centurion who was watching Jesus when He died and say, "Truly this man was the Son of God." Mark 15:39, last part. He is declared to be the Son of God with power, according to the spirit of holiness by the resurrection from the dead. Romans 1:4

The Earthly Ministry of Jesus (Mark 11:7-1) When Jesus rode triumphantly into Jerusalem (vv. 7-11), He was aware that He was making a messianic entry, fulfilling the prophecy of Zechariah 9:9 that the Messiah would someday come into Jerusalem on a donkey. He had sent for the donkey and approved of the messianic shouts of *Hosanna* ("Save now"—Ps. 118:25-26). He had come to live and die as the Christ, to purchase humane redemption (Mark 10:45). Claims that "He was just another Rabbi," or that "He never claimed to be the Messiah, "appear wholly fallacious in light of His claims in the Gospel (e.g., John 8:56-59; 11:23-26). Christ's ministry may be divided into the following eight chronological periods:

(1) *The birth and childhood years.* We have the scriptural account of Jesus' virgin birth (Luke 1:26-38: 2-7), the visit of the wise men, the flight into Egypt (Matt 2:1-23), and His return to dwell in Nazareth. At the age of twelve He astounded the doctors of the Law in the temple (Luke 2:41-47). The other years are not recounted until the beginning of His ministry at the age of thirty (John 2:11).

(2) *The ministry of John the Baptist.* John was the forerunner of Christ, fulfilling Isaiah 40:2-5. He preached repentance and baptized with water, outwardly signifying the inward cleansing. A fearless preacher, he was imprisoned and later beheaded by Herod (Matt. 14:1-12).

(3) *The year of introductions.* Jesus baptism, temptation, and initial teaching ministries in Judea, Jerusalem, Samaria, and Galilee took place during that time.

(4) *The year of popularity.* This was the year of His great Galilean ministry, when He chose the twelve disciples, delivered the Sermon on the Mount, and worked many miracles around Capernaum. Huge crowds eagerly followed Jesus in those days.

(5) *The year of antagonism.* After the feeding of five thousand in Galilee, when He refused to become a political King in opposition to Rome, the huge crowds for the most part deserted Him (John 6:66). He then

began to minister in the Caesarea Philippi region to build the faith of His disciples (Matt. 16:13-16). By this time the leaders at Jerusalem were set against Him, so He avoided overexposure in Jerusalem (John 7:1). He still taught, healed, and did many other good works.

(6) *The final months.* Toward the end of His earthly career, He ministered east of the Jordan River and periodically visited Judea. During this time He raised Lazarus (the brother of Mary and Martha of Bethany) from the dead, thus showing His glory (John 11:1-44).

(7) *The last week.* This week was filled with drama for heaven and earth: His triumphal entry into Jerusalem; His rebuking of the Pharisees and scribes (Matt 23:1-36); His Olivet Discourse on further events (Matt 24:3-51); the Last Supper; His betrayal, arrest, and trials before the high priest, the Sanhedrin, Pilate, Herod, and the mob; and His crucifixion for the sins of mankind on the hill of Calvary (Matt 26:47-68).

(8) *The risen ministry.* After three days He arose from the dead and appeared frequently both in Jerusalem and at the Sea of Galilee to the twelve disciples and to others, "to whom He also presented Himself alive after His suffering to many infallible proofs being seen by them during forty days of speaking of the things pertaining to the kingdom of God" (Acts 1:3).

The Church: Its Beginning and Development (Acts 8:1-8)

After the crucifixion and resurrection of Christ, His church was formed to take the gospel to the lost of all nations. The church went forward with the Good News, and the book of Acts records the two chief events; evangelizing the Jews (Act1-10) and the Gentiles (Act 11-28).

(1) The church was established in Jerusalem and Israel through the following phases:

  (a) *Commissioning.* Soon after Christ arose, He commanded that everyone be evangelized in Jerusalem, Samaria, and among all nations (Acts 1:8).

  (b) *Empowerment.* On the Day of Pentecost, the Holy Spirit came upon the Upper Room congregation of about 120 persons and filled them (Acts 1:15) with power masses, resulting in approximately three thousand conversions (Acts 2:1-44).

  (c) *Witnessing.* The apostle preached, performed miracles, suffered persecution, united in prayer for Holy Spirit power, shared their faith and their worldly goods, and rejoiced that they were counted worthy to suffer shame for His name (Acts 3-5).

(d) *Serving.* The first deacons were chosen by the apostles by laying on of hands, and prayers were commissioned (Acts 6).

(e) *Martyred.* Stephen was the first Christian martyred for preaching the gospel of the Lord Jesus Christ (Acts 7).

(f) *The church persecuted and scattered.* As they went they evangelized, winning, evangelistic crusades (Acts7)

(g) *Conversion of Paul.* Paul, who was then called Saul, was the chief persecutor of the church. He was miraculously converted as he was doing his destructive work (Acts 9).

(h) *Opened doors.* The Gentiles were brought into the church— beginning a great new era of soul-winning and discipling of the Gentiles (Acts 10 and 11).

(i) *Deliverance.* Simon Peter was imprisoned by Herod, That night the angel of the Lord led Peter out of prison and to his Christian friends who were assembled in a church in prayer for his deliverance (Acts 12).

(2) **The church was established among Gentiles**

(a) *By evangelism.* The church at Antioch was ministering to the Lord when the Holy Spirit said, "Now separate to Me Barnabas and Saul for the work to which I have called them" (Acts 12:2). On their three missionary journeys, they were led by the Holy Spirit to evangelize in what is today Turkey and Greece (Acts 13-21).

(b) *By deliverance from legalists.* Paul and Silas journeyed to the Jerusalem council to settle the question once and for all that the Gentiles who had been converted by Christ should not be expected to be burdened with the Jewish ceremonial laws (Acts 15).

(c) *By continuing evangelism.* Paul and Silas took a second missionary journey into the Greek world (Acts 16-18).

(d) *By strengthening.* The third missionary journey, again into Turkey and Greece, edified and strengthened the churches (Acts 22-26).

(e)   *By Paul's chains.* Though Paul was imprisoned in Caesarea, the gospel was not bound (Acts 22-26).

(f)   *By Paul's perilous voyage.* Paul was saved to evangelize in his hazardous voyage to Rome (Acts 27).

(g)   *By divinely opened doors.* Paul's imprisonment in Rome gave him the opportunity to witness and win those who were serving in Rome's palace guard (Acts 28).

The Evangelistic Missionary Journeys of Paul (Acts 13:1-3)

A mission is spreading the Good News that God forgives sinners who trust in Christ. The church sent forth Paul and Barnabas from Antioch of Syria (Rom. 10:15). The first missionaries were sent out by their local church, and were undoubtedly supported by it, as they prayed together seeking God's will for these ministries (vv. 1-3). The apostle Paul and his associates endured extraordinary labors and poverty to give others the message (2 Cor. 11:23-29). There may never have been another who labored so arduously, so long, and under such hardships, with such astonishing success as the brilliant apostle Paul.

(1)   *Paul's calling and commission* (vv. 1-3). Paul and Barnabas were called to evangelize the Gentiles.

(2)   *First missionary journey* (Acts 13 and 14).

(a)   Cyprus—First they evangelized in Barnabas' native land. Saul became known by his Greek name, Paul, John and Mark deserted them and returned to Jerusalem.

(b)   Pisidia (Turkey)—Next they evangelized Paul's native land. They preached the gospel in Antioch, Iconium, Lystram and Derne. They were persecuted everywhere, but some believed.

(c)   They returned to Antioch of Syria and reported to the church (Acts 14:24-28).

(3)   *Jerusalem council* (Acts 15).

(a)   Paul and Barnabas participated with the leaders of the church in seeking God's will regarding the relation of the ceremonial law to the Gentiles.

(b)   The question of circumcision and ceremonial law was solved
at the Jerusalem council, decreeing that it was God's will that
Gentiles be fully and equally admitted into the church, with
having the duty to obey the Jewish ceremonial laws (Acts
15:22-29).

(4) *Second missionary journey* (Acts 16:1-18:22).

(a)   Paul and Barnabas separated, but the work continued. Paul
took Silas on the second journey.
(b)   The churches started on the first journey were revisited (Acts
15:41). This is our example to nurture new converts.
(c)   In a vision, Paul was guided to enter Europe (Acts 16:9-10).
Lydia was the first convert in Europe (Acts 16:14).
(d)   They witnessed in the great Greek cities of Philippi,
Thessalonica, Athens, Corinth, and Ephesus.
(e)   They returned to Antioch of Syria and informed the church
of their journeys.

(5) *Third missionary journey* (Acts 18:23-21:16)

(a)   The churches which had been started by Paul were revisited
(b)   Paul taught in Ephesus for three years and displayed flexibility
in staying at a location when opportunity or need arose.
(c)   He revisited the various Greek cities as well as Jerusalem.

(6) *Witnessed in Jerusalem* (Acts 21:17-23:32). God gave Paul opportunity
to witness to the high priest and the Sanhedrin.
(7) *Caesarean imprisonment* (Acts 23:31—26:32). God gave Paul the
opportunity to witness rulers of the land: the governors Felix and
Festus, and King Agrippa II.
(8) *Voyage to Rome* (Acts 27). God preserved His servants to continue in
their work.
(9) *Roman imprisonment* (Acts 28:16-31). God gave Paul opportunity
to witness to the Jewish community in Rome and to many great
personages of the Roman Empire.
(10) *Final travels* (Rom. 15:24). Paul expressed his desire to witness in
Spain.

(11) *Second Roman imprisonment and martyrdom.* The witnesses in Spain are uniform in their testimony that Paul was martyred in Rome by Nero.

The Fall of Jerusalem and the End of the First Century
(Hebrews 3:12-19)

This passage speaks of those who wandered forty years in the wilderness and, because of their lack of faith, never entered God's rest in Canaan. Similarly, after the Jerusalem religious leaders rejected Christ, God gave them forty years of apostolic preaching to change their minds and accept Him. When the majority did not believe, approximately forty years after the Crucifixion the Romans destroyed Jerusalem (AD 70). Thus, Jesus told the women of Jerusalem who were weeping as He went to the cross, "Do not weep for Me, but weep for yourselves" (Luke 23:28-29). He went on to speak of the suffering, which was ahead for the city, because it was cutting itself off from God's help by crucifying God the Son.

Baptism

Scriptural Teachings: 1 Corinthians 15:1-4; 32 1 Thessalonians 4:13-18; Mark 28:19; Romans 10-10; Mark 1:19-10; Romans 6:1-10; Matthew 28:18, 19; Acts 8:35-39, 1 Corinthians 11:2, 26-29.

Baptism is performed by dipping or immersing a believer in water in the name of the Father, Son and Holy Ghost. All believers should be baptized upon a profession of their faith in Christ. We are baptized upon a profession of our faith representing a regeneration of forgiveness. Christ has commanded us to declare our faith in Him by being baptized.

Baptism signifies three things:

1. your salvation was made possible by the death, burial, and resurrection of Jesus Christ
2. you are dead to sin and have arisen to walk in the newness of life
3. you have a hope of the resurrection of the body from the grave at the second coming of Jesus.

Baptism is an ordinance (a set practice ordered to be done) of the Church. There are two ordinances of the church, Baptism and the Lord's Supper.

The Lord's Supper

Hebrews 9:22, Matthew 26:26-30; 1 Corinthians 11:23-26

The Lord's Supper is a church ordinance, a feast of bread and wine participated in by baptized members of the church who are living orderly before the world. The Lord's Supper was instituted by our Saviour on the night before he was crucified. It signifies the atoning death of Christ : the bread represents his body and the wine, his blood.

Christ was born to die. Without His blood there could be no forgiveness of sin, Christ the perfect Son of God became the Lamb of God. When Christ said of the bread, "This is my body," He meant that it represented His body. The "cup" represented the blood of Christ shed on The Calvary for ratification of the "New Testament." To eat the bread and drink the cup means to proclaim and accept the benefits of Christ' sacrificial death.

Each person should examine himself to see if he is in the faith and decide his fitness to partake of the Lord's Supper before he does so. It is better not to partake if one is not fit, and yet one should not feel that he is unfit if he knows he is born again and is walking as he should be "in the gospel".

Organization: Have a Plan

The fatal flaw in most plans and methods of work is that they are not carried out. We fail to see things accomplished not because they are unworkable, but because they are not worked! A method of study is only a guide to work. Find a method of study that works for you and stick to it. It is also helpful for you to know how to expand your study if you need to. Know where you can go for more material to look at, such as a library. Discuss your finding with someone, and listen to their response. This can help you avoid foolish and unlearned questions (2 Tim 2:23.) After the plan is made, the work remains to be done.

The difficulty is not the lack of time. It is the lack of coordination in the use of time. If you are failing to plan, then you are planning to fail. Start with a simple plan that works for you and stick with it. Make up your mind to spend some time *every day* studying God's Word. Remember, Bible study is one of the most fruitful resolutions that a Christian can make. It can be the turning point in your life, and can change it from barren and unfruitful to rich and rewarding.

This change can only be accomplished through faithful, persevering, daily study of the Bible. This study may not be very interesting at first, but you will soon begin to see that the more time you spend on God's Word, the more you will come to love it and the more it will enrich your life.

Be sure that you set aside a certain allotted time to study. You choose the time to study. Do not allow other things to interrupt your study. If you can, try to give more than fifteen minutes a day to Bible Study. Whenever possible, lock yourself in with God alone.

Be realistic. Sit down and figure out how much time you spend doing other things, like watching TV, reading the newspaper, talking on the phone, going to the mall, or whatever it is that you do during a normal week. Then add up the time that you have used (Do not forget to add sleeping and eating). Remember that everybody has 24 hours in each day. This breaks down to 1,440 minutes.

Always Keep the Bible As the Center of Your Study

You can (and should) use other books as you study, but always remember to keep the Bible as the center of your study. You may find it helpful to use other translations of the Scriptures in your study of God's Word. They may help enrich your study time as one version often explains another. This is particularly helpful when you are having difficulty understanding a verse or passage.

Tragedy of the Church Member

Text—"he that putteth his hand to the plow and looketh back is not fit for The kingdom of God."—Luke 9:62

The supreme tragedy of the church member is not his succumbing to temptation, or his sins. It is being made unfit for the kingdom of God by choosing to remain in a state of sin. It is the voluntary surrender of man to temptation and sin as determined by destiny. Let me be more explicit. When a person becomes a member of the church, he takes a solemn vow, just like he does when he is made a citizen of a country. If the citizen breaks his vow, he is a traitor. When persons are united in marriage, they take a solemn vow. If they break that vow, they commit adultery.

When a man gives testimony before a court of justice, he takes an oath to tell the truth. If that person says anything that is not true, he or she commits perjury. Treason, adultery, and perjury are great sins against the state, the home and justice.

But solemn as these vows are, not one of them is as solemn as the one taken in church membership, nor are they as far reaching. For after declaring belief in God, the Father, in Jesus Christ, the Savior and the Holy Sprit, the Guide, the candidate then solemnly says "I renounce the devil and all his works and ways, and accept the Holy Spirit in faith and obedience unto the end,"

That is the eternal vow. For a person to take that vow before God and then to repudiate it deliberately, and to abandon his publicly declared purpose to follow God, is to, my mind, the greatest tragedy of human life. It seems hardly possible that any intelligent person should be guilty of such a sin. We can put a prop under a weak limb of a tree and save it from breaking, but what can be done after it has broken off?

Tragedy of the Church Member

The situation is like this at home. Suppose there are ten children in this particular home. There is also a large farm and lots of work to be done. The expense of upkeep is very considerable, but by thrift and co-operation it is all provided and the family is happy and contented. But by and by one quits because he is offended, another because of jealously, another because of pride, another becomes wayward, and another because of impurity and so on until there are only a few left. By this time, the glory of the home is gone. The love is also gone. No more happiness; the property is neglected for the lack of help. The question becomes "Why did they not adjust their affairs in a satisfactory manner to all and keep the home intact and save the home and the hearts from breaking?"

It could have been done. It should have been done. Apply this to the church family and see how many a church is broken up and the heart of Jesus broken afresh because of the conduct of church members.

1. The apostate church member is a tragedy to himself. He forgot the injunction of Shakespeare, "This above all: to thine own self be true and thou canst not then be false to any man."

    a. He breaks a covenant with God and man, thus proving that morally he has collapsed. He has lost the dignity of manhood and acts more like a jellyfish than a man.

b. He does dishonor to the most solemn word of honor that he ever uttered. Failing here, how can men trust him in lesser things?

c. He breaks the golden cord of faith, blasts a noble purpose, crucifies his will, paralyzes his conscience and lies to the Holy Spirit. He either proves that he has never been converted and has thereby been living a deceitful, hypocritical life, or that he has been deceiving himself about his union with God, or

d. He has sinned for which there is no repentance as set forth in Hebrew 6:4-9. "For it is impossible for those who were once enlightened, and have tasted of the heavenly gift, and were made partakers of the Holy Ghost, and having tasted to go to the Word of God, and the powers of the world to come, if they fall away, to renew them again into repentance; seeing they fall crucify to themselves, the Son of God afresh, and put Him to an open shame." Hebrew 10:26-31, "For if we sin willfully after that we have received knowledge of the truth, there remaineth no more sacrifice for sins, but a certain looking for of judgment and fiery indignation, which shall devour the adversaries. He that despised Moses law died without mercy under two or three witness: Of how sorer punishment, suppose ye, shall he be thought worthy, who hath trodden underfoot the Son of God, and hath counted the blood of the covenant, wherewith he was sanctified, an unholy thing, and hath done despite unto the sprite of Grace?—it is a fearful thing to fall into the hands of the living God."

2. The apostate church member is a tragedy to the church. Not only is he personally involved, but the church of Christ also. The institution which God has placed here in the world to remind men of sin and to call them to Himself for salvation.

a. He causes the church to be unjustly accused of weakness, of protecting hypocrites. He brings the church into a bad light by making her the subject of contempt and suspicion.

b. By his actions, he keeps many people out of the church. He hurts the influence of the church in the community. For he is still recognized as a member and when he dies his folk will expect a Christian funeral service for him.

    c.   He mocks the church by neglecting to attend services, by open defiance and by showing personal contempt for high and holy ideals. That hurts the church like it hurts a mother to have her son say to her that she is disreputable, whether it is true or not. It is like calling a mother a prostitute.

    d.   He would destroy the entire fabric of the organization of the church if his following were large enough. He would do this by his acts and words. But God sees to it that such persons have limited influence.

    e.   He is a dead limb on a healthy tree.

3.   The apostate church member is a tragedy to Christ. Surely, one of the saddest things in the life of Christ on earth must have been denial of Peter and the betrayal by Judas. How His great yearning heart broke when He saw his men turn from Him. It breaks His heart just the same way today when He sees unfaithful followers. He died of a broken heart. Why do we continue to crucify Him afresh? To turn our backs upon the church is to turn our backs upon Christ. Christ and the church are one. He is the Head, the church is His body. The church is His bride. He wants to present His Bride before the Father, a glorious church, not having a spot, or wrinkle, or any such thing; but that it should be whole and without blemish. To be unfaithful to Him and His church is to repeat the tragedy on Calvary.

4.   The apostate church member is a tragedy to humanity. It is a terrible manifestation of the weakness of the flesh; it shows how inconstant man is. It shows how unworthy he is of the Divine love of God. It shows how low a man can fall and how content he may be to lie down there.

    a.   He is an example for other church members to follow; everybody has some following.

    b.   And because of his hypocrisy, many people will never seek the church of Christ as a haven for their souls.

    c.   He will be the cause of the wrath of God falling not only upon himself but upon members of the family and others.

This is not an indictment upon any one. It is a part of a pastor's responsibility to preach the whole Word; it is the warning from the man on the watchtower who sees the enemy approaching. It is the flash of the passion of one who is trying to feed the flock of God, to tend to his sheep. It is a call of warning to prevent any one from betraying His Lord, and the call to any one who may be slipping away to come back home to God, to come back into the church, to return to faith and service. "Take heed lest any of you be hardened through the deceitfulness of sin." We know what the will of God is in this matter. We know too how we stand with Him. We know God wants us to do His will. We know that He will help us if we will do our part. Now is our opportunity to do a really great work for God in the churches of this community. Let us line up solid for our faith. Let us get right with God ourselves, then we can teach transgressors the way.

Let us put our hand to the plow and not even look back so that we may be fit for the Kingdom of God.

The Tribulation on the Earth

"Then they will deliver you up to tribulation and kill you, and you will be hated by all nations for My name's sake." Matt. 10:17

The Tribulation on the Earth (Matthew 24:9-30)

(1)   It will be a period of God's wrath. Christ describes a time of great tribulation (pressure, agony, suffering) on the earth (vv. 21, 22), during which Christ will let loose three successive series of judgment: the seven deals (Rev. 6:1-17; 8:1), the seven trumpets (Rev. 8:7-9:21, 11:15-19), and the seven bowls of God's wrath (Rev, 15, 16). Since God will be pouring out His wrath on a wicked and rebellious earth (Rev. 6:17), it is fitting to note that "God did not appoint us to wrath" (1 Thess. 5:9).

(2)   It will last seven years. Christ refers us to Daniel 9:27 for the length of this period, which is set forth as seven years—one "week" of years (v.15),

(3)   It will begin with the signing of the covenant. "He [the Antichrist, who will come out of the revived Roman Empire] shall confirm a covenant with many" (Dan. 9:27).

(4)   The Antichrist will set up the "abomination of desolation". In the middle of the seven years (v.15; Dan. 9-27). This will be a dreadful, public sin perpetrated in Jerusalem at the rebuilt temple (2 Thess. 2:3-4). This prophesized abomination could not have been Titus' destruction of the temple in AD 70

because those actions do not fit either 2 Thessalonians 2:3-4, nor events described in Matthew 24:22, 29. Clearly, it is a future event.

(5) The abomination will start a fierce persecution. This final three-and-one half years period is the actual time of "great tribulation" (v.21), although the entire seven years are commonly so labeled. Verse 21 describes the ferocity of this period. The book of Revelation shows that it will be a satanic attack against Israel and all those from the nations who turn to Christ (Rev. 7:9-14; 12:13, 15; cf. Zech, 12:2-3; 14:2).

(6) The Antichrist will reign during the last three-and one-half years (Rev. 13:5), leading his beast empire (the revived Roman Empire, in ten confederate states). During this period, God and Satan will war with one another: God's anger (Rev. 6:17) will be roused against Satan's persecution of "the woman [Israel] who gave birth to the male Child [Christ]" (Rev. 12:11-13).

(7) The Tribulation will close at Armageddon (Rev. 16:16-17)

The Judgment of the Wicked (Revelation 20:11-15)—The Great White Throne judgment will follow the thousand-year reign of Christ. This is the final judgment, and only the wicked dead are to be judged. According to Revelation 20:5, believers were resurrected a thousand years before this judgment. Their works were judged at the "judgment seat of Christ" (2 Cor. 5:10).

(1) At this judgment the wicked dead will seek a hiding place from the face of the Lord Jesus Christ, the Judge. But there is no hiding place.

(2) At this judgment the "dead, small and great" (v. 12), will stand before God. But the greatness of the great will be of no value. "There is none who does good, no, not one" (Rom. 3:12).

(3) At this judgment the "Book of Life" (v.12) will be opened to show conclusively that these people are not in the Lamb's Book of Life.

(4) At this judgment the dead will be judged "each one according to his works" (v.13). God is a just God, and since there are degrees of punishment in hell, some will be punished more than others (Luke 12:42-48).

(5) At this judgment, there will be no acquittal, no higher court to which the losers may appeal; they are lost, and lost forever, they are damned

to all eternity, without hope. In hell there is no hope, no sympathy, and no love. Even the love of God does not extend into the portals of hell.

JUSTIFICATION

The word "justify" means to be just (or righteous) before God. (Romans 2:13,] "to be made righteous" (Romans 5:18-19), "to establish as right," "to set or put right" It denoted being in a right relationship with God. The Bible teaches us that God justifies a sinner in treating him as "just" for Christ' sake. Justification is God's act of declaring us "not guilty" for our sins.

SANCTIFICATION

Sanctification as used in the Scriptures means to make holy, to consecrate, to separate from the world and be set apart from sin in order that we may have a close fellowship with God and serve Him. The Bible teaches that to sanctify is to make holy in heart and in life (Leviticus 11:44; Leviticus 20:7; Leviticus 8, Exodus 19:9-22; Matthew 22:37, 1 Thessalonians 4:3, 4). Sanctification requires that believers:

1. maintain an intimate communion with Christ (John 15;4)
2. engage in fellowship with believers (Ephesians 4:15-16).
3. devote themselves to prayer (Matthew 6:15-13; Colossians 4:2)
4. obey God's word (John 17:17)
5. be sensitive to the presence and care of God (Matthew 6:25-34)
6. love righteousness and hate iniquity (Hebrews 1:9).
7. put sin to death (Romans 6)
8. submit to God's discipline (Hebrews 12:5-11)
9. continue to obey and be filled with the Holy Ghost (Romans 8:14)

FAITH

By faith in Christ, in the Scriptures, means believing Christ to be the Divine Savior and personally trusting in Him for our salvation. Faith in Jesus as Lord and Savior is both the act of a single moment and a continuing attitude for life that must grow and be strengthened (John 1:12). Because we have faith in a definite person who died for us (Romans 4:25; 8:32; 1 Thessalonians 1:3; Peter 1:3-9), our faith should become greater (Romans 4:20; 2 Thessalonians 1:3, 1 Peter 1. 3-9).

SALVATION

Salvation means, "being saved", "deliverance" "bring safely through" "keeping from harm". It is described in the Bible as "the way" or road that leads through life to eternal fellowship with God in heaven. The Bible teaches us that Jesus Christ is the Savior of men. Christ is the salvation of the world.

God freely offers us eternal life in Jesus Christ. But understanding the exact process used to make that available to us is sometimes difficult for us to grasp. Therefore God presents various pictures in the Bible for salvation, each one with its own unique emphasis.

Christ is the way to the Father (John 14:5; Acts 4:12). Salvation is provided for us by God's grace which He gives in Christ Jesus (Roman 3:24), based on His death (Romans 3:25; Romans 5:8), the Resurrection (Romans 5:10), and continued intercession for believers (Hebrews 7:25).

Salvation is received by grace, through faith in Christ (Romans 3:22, 24-25, 26). That is, it comes as a result of God's grace (John 1:16) and the human response of faith (Acts 16:31; Romans 1:17; Ephesians 1:15; 2:8).

Salvation includes the personal experience by which we as believers receive forgiveness of sins (Acts 10:43; Romans 4:6-8) and pass from spiritual death to spiritual life (1 John 3:14), from the power of sin to the power of the Lord, (Romans 6:17-23) from the dominion of Satan to the dominion of God (Acts 26:18). It brings us into a new personal relationship with God (John 1:12) and rescues us from the penalty of sin (Romans 1:16; 6; 23; 1 Corinthians 1:18).

REPENTANCE

What is meant by repentance of sin? The basic meaning of repentance is "to turn around": It is a turning from evil ways and a turning to Christ, and through Him to God (John 14:1, 6: Acts 8:22, 26:18; 1 Peter 2:25). Repentance is a free decision on the part of the sinner, made possible by the enabling grace given to him as he hears and believes the gospel.

Tithing

Scripture Readings: Genesis 14:20; Leviticus 27:30, Malachi 3:8; Amos 4:4; Matthew 23:23; Luke 7:47: Luke 16:11: Luke 18:12; I1 Corinthians 16:2: Romans 1:14-15; 2 Corinthians 8:5; 2 Corinthians 8:14

Tithing is the practice of giving God a tenth of one's income. It is a moral and spiritual obligation of the Christian for the following reasons:

1. Our gifts indicate our love for God.
2. Our gifts indicate our interest in the extension of God's kingdom
3. Our gifts indicate where our treasure is
4. Our gifts indicate whether God or mammon is first in life
5. Our gifts indicate whether we are being obedient to God
6. Our gifts indicate whether we are trying to be faithful stewards
7. Our gifts indicate whether our heart is in the work of the Lord or not.

An increase of faith in all of the promises of God is one of the rich fruits of the practice of tithing. All of us agree that a greater faith in God is indeed a rich blessing. Many have discovered that when they begin to trust God with their money they found it easier to trust God in other areas of life. The practice of tithing permits God to prove His divine trustworthiness. God honors His promises. The Bible is a book of promises and the Christian's faith will be greater when these promises are discovered and claimed by faith.

If you are a consistent thither and God has blessed your heart in so doing, when the opportunity presents itself bear your testimony for the glory of God and the strengthening of the faith of someone who needs encouragement to trust God more fully in his economic life.

If you have not yet discovered the joy of being a tither, we would challenge you to become a tither. If you do not have faith to make the full decision then take a step in the right direction, and begin by increasing your regular contribution today.

Examples of Tithing:

Gross (before deductions) weekly income: $430.00 Tithing amount $43.00 per week or $172.00 a month

Gross (before deductions) weekly income: $4300.00 Tithing amount $430.00 per week.

Gross (before deductions) bi-weekly (every 2 weeks) income: $430.00 Tithing amount $43.00 every two weeks.

Daniel

The book of Daniel is the most astounding of all the Old Testament prophets. The personal life of Daniel is hard to rival with its extremes of danger and advancement, and the prophecies of Daniel are the best summaries to be found in the Bible of God's plan for human history.

Although twenty-six centuries separate Daniel from us today, we are bombarded with the cruelty and turmoil of wars, threatened wars, political transitions, and ruthless despots. All of this is illustrated during Daniel's life and foretold in his prophetic writings. As a teen-age exile from Jerusalem in 605 BC, Daniel must have experienced a ruptured family, personal suffering, humiliation, and despair. Yet his faith, prayer life, national leadership, and prophetic insight are honored and no incident of sin or weakness is recorded.

Many Christians pay minimal attention to Gentile nations, focusing their attention instead on God's chosen people, Israel. However, the Scriptures include reference to the tides of Gentiles who periodically overflowed into Israel, whether for temporary association, alliance, or total conquest. In the book of Daniel, these nations are noted historically and then become the pattern for future instances of wickedness, covetousness, and blasphemy toward the God of Israel.

AUTHORSHIP

The book of Daniel is the last of the four Major Prophets of the Old Testament (the other three being Isaiah, Jeremiah, and Ezekiel). In the Hebrew Bible, however, Daniel is not found in the second section to the Biblical canon (the Prophets) but in the third section (the Writings). The canon of the Prophets was closed about 200 BC, and some modern scholars argue that this indicates Daniel was written under Antiochus Epiphanies, a Seleucid (Greek) ruler who reigned from about 175 BC to about 163 BC

According to this view, the book of Daniel was penned by an anonymous writer (or writers) who used the respected figure of Daniel (Ezek. 14:14, 20: 28:3) to lend authority, credence and persuasive power to their composition. Their purpose was to support the faith of the Jews during the terrible persecution then raging under Antiochus Epiphanies and to encourage them to remain courageous and steadfast even in the face of martyrdom because the book does not mention the cleansing of the temple, which took place under Judas Maccabeus in December 165 BC. These scholars suggest that the book was written sometime between 168 and 165 BC. This theory has found widespread support.

As plausible and convincing as the theory may appear, however, it has one fatal flaw. The basic reason why some scholars deny the genuineness of Daniel's authorship is that they have rejected the possibility of predictive prophecy, Denying that an omniscient God could have revealed future events to Daniel or any other prophet, they claim that all "prophecy" is actually written after the historical events have occurred.

Conservative scholars reject such rationalistic skepticism about the Biblical text and believe that the author of the book of Daniel was indeed the prophet Daniel who lived during the time of Nebuchadnezzar, Belshazzar, Cyrus, and Darius. By the revelation of God, Daniel was able to see events that were to transpire hundreds of years in the future, to envision the fall of the empires that had not yet arisen on the world scene. It would indeed have been impossible for Daniel to pen such a chronicle of future events on his own; but, as our Lord Jesus Christ said, "The things which are impossible with men are possible with God" (Luke 118:27).

KEY VERSES: 2:20-22, 44

"Daniel answered and said: 'Blessed be the name of God forever and ever for wisdom and might are His. And He changes the times and the seasons; He removes kings and raises up kings; He gives wisdom to the wise and knowledge to those who have understanding, He reveals deep and secret things; He knows what is in the darkness, and light dwells with Him.' . . . 'And in the days of these kings the God of heaven will set up a kingdom which shall never be destroyed; and the kingdom shall not be left to other people; it shall break in pieces and consume all these kingdoms, and it shall stand forever."

The principle idea of the book of Daniel is the ultimate triumph of the kingdom of God. The book contains prophecies of the nations of the world and of Israel's future in relation to them in the sovereign plan of God. Throughout world history a succession of empires rise, have their day of glory and power, and then fall. When their allotted time span is fulfilled, they are overthrown. The wicked rulers and nations that shake their fist at the Almighty wind up on the ash heap if history; those who abide in righteousness and faithfulness to the Lord, even though they were persecuted and even martyred, will receive their ultimate reward: "And many of those who sleep in the dust of the earth shall awake, soon to everlasting contempt" (12:2). Nowhere in the Old Testament is the Christian doctrine of resurrection more clearly enunciated than in this verse.

HOW DANIEL FITS TOGETHER

After a lengthy historical introduction describing the education of Daniel and his friends Shadrach, Meshach and Abed-Nego (ch.1), the book of Daniel falls into two clearly distinct parts: (1) events and prophecies concerning the nations of earth, their character, relations, succession, and destiny (Chs. 2-6) and (2) a collection of visions describing the Hebrew nation, its relations to Gentile dominion, and its future in the plan of God (7-12).

The first part of the book contains five sections: (a) Nebuchadnezzar's dream of a great image: a prophecy of "the times of the Gentiles" (Luke 21:24), when Israel would be ruled by Gentile powers (2:1-49); (b) Nebuchadnezzar's trail of the confessors' faith-the image of gold and the deliverance from the fiery furnace: a lesson in steadfast faith (3:1-30); (c) Nebuchadnezzar's vision of a tree whose height reached to the heavens and his afflictions and humiliation: a lesson in humanity (4:1-37); (d) Belshazzar's drunken feast and Daniel's interpretation of the handwriting on the wall: a lesson in sin and its punishment (5:1-31); and (e) Darius the Mede in the role of unwilling religious persecutor, and the plot against Daniel and his deliverance in the lions' den, a lesson in faith, prayer and courage in the face of persecution (6:1-28).

The second part of the book, a collection of visions seen by Daniel, contains four visions: (a) a vision of four beasts, the Ancient of Days, and the Son of Man: the conflict of Christ with the Antichrist (7:1-28); (b) visions of a ram, a goat, and a little horn: Israel's conflict with Antiochus Epiphanies, the Old Testament foreshadowing of the future Antichrist (8:1-27); (c) a vision of the seventy weeks and Daniel's prayer for his people: Israel's future in the plan of the God (9:1-27); and (d) a final vision of Israel through the centuries, and the consummation in the hands of enemies and in the hands of God: a prophecy of the end of time (10;1-12:13).

Daniel's prophecies are first panoramic (e.g., Chs. 2 and 7), and then more specific. Chapter 9 contains probably the most definitive Old Testament prophecy of the time of our Lord's first advent, the period between the sixty-ninth and seventieth "week" which allows for the present church age, the duration of the Great Tribulation, and the menace of the Antichrist. Chapters

11-12 give us further insight into the culmination of human rebellion against God, and the blessed promise of resurrection for these who are loyal to Christ in the midst of world apostasy and the conflagration called Armageddon.

The book of Daniel will not be clear to everyone. The casual reader will simply skim the surface and benefit little. The spiritually indifferent reader will conclude with frightening details and problem passages which precipitate arguments. The key to understanding is to begin with Daniel's prayer of 9:1-19. It may be the most overlooked prayer of penitence in the Bible. It created the proper view of the relations between God and His backslidden people. Daniel identified with Israel's wickedness, confesses it, and pleads with God for his response in forgiveness for His own glory. God answered Daniel's prayer by giving him revelation and insight.

Let the spirit of this prayer enable the reader to claim the help of the Holy Spirit in understanding the astounding revelation of the future.

History, Prophecy, and Biography (Daniel 1:1-21) "In the third year of the reign of Jehoiakim, King of Judah [606 BC], Nebuchadnezzar, King of Babylon came to Jerusalem, and besieged it "(v.1) . . .], Nebuchadnezzar had defeated the Egyptian army and was moving to besiege Jerusalem, an event that marked the beginning of the fall of Jerusalem and the seventy years of Babylonian captivity (vv. 1,2). It was also the beginning of "the time of the Gentiles" (Luke 21:24), which is to continue through the seven years of the Great Tribulation called "the time of Jacob's trouble "(Jer.30: 7). The final assault in the city of Jerusalem came during the reign of Zedekiah, Judah's last king. Jeremiah, the prophet, prophesied the end of Judah and Jerusalem (Jer 21:1), The prophecy was fulfilled, and then recorded by Jeremiah (Jer, 52:1-34).

(1)   Three figurehead kings: the last three monarchs of Judah were puppet kings Jehoiakim who reigned for eleven years (2 Kin. 23:36-24:5, 2 Chr. 36:5-8); Jehoiachin, his son, who reigned for three months (2 Kin. 24.8, 9); and Zedekiah, who ruled for eleven years (2 Kin. 35:17-25:7; 2 Char 36:10-13). All three kings were evil in the sight of God, who accordingly brought judgment upon them, sending Nebuchadnezzar to take the people into captivity in Babylon and to burn the city of Jerusalem. Jehoiakim was so evil Jeremiah prophesied that upon his death the king would be given the burial of a donkey (Jer. 22:18, 19). Jehoiachin, after serving thirty-seven years as a prisoner, was given his freedom and finally exalted by Evil-Merodach, king of Babylon. In

his first year, the Babylonians (Jer. 52:31-34) Zedekiah did not fare so well. The king of Babylon brutally killed Zedekiah's son before his very eyes, and then blinded him. The last thing this wicked king saw was the brutal execution of his son. He must have carried that picture in his mind until the day he died in a Babylonian prison (Jer. 52:10).

(2) Four courageous young Hebrews, Daniel, Hannaniah, Mishael, and Azariah of royal blood, descendants of godly Hezekiah (vv. 3-7), were chosen by God to know His will for their lives (Acts 22:13, 14). About a hundred years before Judah was taken captive to Babylon, Isaiah had prophesied that Hezekiah's descendants would be made eunuchs in the palace of the king of Babylon (Is. 39:5-7). Daniel and his companions were of the spiritual nobility of the Hebrew captives. They were selected by Ashpenaz (master of Nebuchadnezzar's eunuchs) to become eunuchs. But unlike others, who compromised and conformed to the Babylonian system, the four young believers were sustained by the power of God. They took their stand for Him, and God stood with them and gave them victory (v. 8; Ch 1 John 5:4). They dared to do the will of God in a pagan land filled with false gods. In Babylon they were tested by Satan's world system (41 John 2:15, 16).

(a) *The lust of the flesh.* The king changed their food, but not their faith. They were appointed a daily provision of the king's meat, and of the wine which he drank (v.5). This was food and drink that was contrary to Hebrew dietary laws (Lev. 11:1-80.) "But Daniel purposed in his heart that he would not defile himself with the portion of the king's delicacies, nor with the wine" (v. 8), Daniel's three Hebrew friends agreed: if God's children would dare to take this stand for Christ, and practice righteousness, God would bless their obedience and bend His enemies to His will (vv. 9-16). After three years of vegetables and water, God gave the young men superior knowledge and skill in all learning and wisdom. The king found them ten times better than all the wise men of the palace (vv. 17-20).

(b) *Lust of the eye.* The Babylonians had changed their country of residence but not the character of the young men (vv. 2, 4). The four young Hebrews were in a strange land filled with pagan gods, steeped in immorality and idolatry (ex. 20:1-6), Babylon was very beautiful and magnificent, especially in its architecture. Its hanging gardens were considered among the seven wonders of the world. It is easy to understand how the eyes of most men (1 John 2:15) would be filled with lust. Satan made Babylon pleasant to behold, But Daniel, Hannaniah, Misheal, and Azariah did not conform to the Babylonian way of life, Transformed by the power of God, they would "prove what is that good and acceptable and perfect will of God" (Rom. 12:1,2).

(c)   ***The pride of life.*** The Babylonians had changed the names of the young men, but nut their nature (vv. 6, 7). It is evident that they were partakers of the divine nature of God (2 Pet. 1:4), and were new creatures in the Messiah (2 Cor. 5:17). They were devoted students of the Old Testament books already by the time of their captivity, not of the learning of Babylon. After reading Isaiah, they looked for the promised Messiah, who would be crucified, wounded for man's transgressions, bruised for his iniquities, and brought as a lamb to slaughter (Is. 53:1-12). When John the Baptist saw Jesus, he said, "Behold! The Lamb of God, who takes away the sins of the world "(John 1:29). John had learned this great truth from the Old Testament, and it was there for Daniel and his friends to learn. Looking back to Calvary saved them. They were given names that honored false gods, but they did not honor their new names.

We learn, then, that it does not matter what you are called; it is what you are in Christ that counts. The Babylonians changed those young men's food, their country, and their names; but Daniel and his friends remained the same in faith, character, and nature. Babylon cold not change them, but they made many changes in Babylon: they even converted Nebuchadnezzar (Dan 4).

The Vision of the Angel in Linen (Daniel 10:1-21)

Daniel, chapters 10-12, is one complete vision in three parts. (Daniel's pagan name, in the courts of Babylon and Persia, was Belteshazzar meaning, "the god Bel is strong." However, from his daily walk everyone realized that his real name was Daniel, "God is my judge.") This vision came to

Daniel in the third year of Cyrus, 536 BC. It was a true vision of coming events. "The appointed time was long" (v.1). Chapters 11 and 12 cover the history of the Gentiles from the Medes and Persians to the coming kingdom of God.

(1) In Daniel's vision he saw himself "by the side of the great river, that is, the Tigris, where he saw "certain man clothed in linen" (vv.4-9), quite possibly our Lord Jesus Christ. The vision was an Old Testament Christophany, or appearance of Christ. In Daniel we have an Old Testament Christophany, and in the book of Revelation (1:9-18) we have a New Testament Christophany which embraces Christ's death, burial, and Resurrection.

(2) "Then, suddenly, a hand touched me" (v.10). The pre-incarnate Christ was not alone in this vision. It was the manifestation of an angel, perhaps Gabriel. The angel was sent by the Lord to answer Daniel's prayer on the first day that he prayed. Gabriel was hindered by "the prince of the kingdom of Persia" (v.13) who delayed him for twenty-one days until Michael (God's warring angel) could come and help him defeat the evil prince-Satan, or one of his fallen angels from the kingdom of darkness (Eph. 6:12). Christ, the Man in linen, did not need Michael to fight His battle and defeat Satan. When He was tested in the wilderness, He met Satan in his own kingdom of darkness and was victorious (Matt. 4:1-11)-for prayer can produce actions behind the scenes (vv.12, 13). Yet there occurred a struggle for twenty-one days (v.13), and from this we can each learn patience through the power of prayer. God hears and He works according to His will. He is accomplishing many things in the lives of men and nations. He requires us to wait many days, but prayer is always answered.

(3) Angels are assigned to watch over God's people. The words, "Michael, your prince" (v.21) show that there exists an assigned bond between certain people and/or nations and God's angels (Heb. 1:14).

(4) It is God's will that both His Old Testament people, Israel and His New Testament people, the church, should "understand what will happen to "them in the latter days" (vv.14, 21). Prophecy should not be ignored, for it can give us stability during difficult days (Matt. 24:6). We should know that whatever happens to us personally or as a nation, God triumphs, as do we as His ransomed children, in the near future (Rev. 3:11; Rev 22:12, 17).

The Vision of the Angel's Oath (Daniel 12:1-13)

This wonderful book of prophecy closes with another Christophany (a pre-incarnate appearance of the glorious Christ). "I heard the man clothed in linen" who "swore by Him who lives forever" (v.7; Heb. 6:13). A great lesson from this book is that God, His Word, and His Christ live on forever, that evil and its satanic forces will one day be removed for eternity. Praise God for His grace that brought Jesus to bear our sins, that we too might one day abide by His side always.

(1) The main events of the end (vv. 1-3):

    (a)   "Michael" shall "stand up . . . [for] the sons of your people" (v.1). This refers to the future. Revelation 12:7-10 describes Michael warring with Satan and casting him out of heaven, as Satan makes his final attempt to destroy Israel and the Tribulation saints-those who believe on Christ during the final seven years (Rev. 12:13).

    (b)   It shall be "a time of trouble, such as never was since there was a nation" v.1).Christ said there "will be great tribulation" (Matt. 24:21, 22; cf. Rev 7:13, 14).

    (c)   "Your people shall be delivered" (v.1). So states Revelation 12:11, 14-16, as well as Zechariah 12:9; 13:9, and 14:3, 4.

    (d)   The dead will be resurrected (v.2). This is the clearest Old Testament testimony to the Resurrection. It was pronounced in its absolute fullness only after Christ Himself conquered the grave and death for us forever (Rev. 1:18, cf. 1 Cor. 15:35-44).

    (e)   There will be rewards for 144,000 from the twelve tribes of the children of Israel, as well as for a great host of Gentiles who will evangelize the nations during the Tribulation, having turned many to righteousness, in heaven they will shine "like the stars forever and ever" (v. 3; cf. Rev 7:1-17). Saved souls of all denominations will receive a special reward in heaven (1 Thess. 2:19, 20).

(2) A sealed book until the end (v.4):

    (a)   "The words are closed up and sealed" (v.9). Until Christ came and the New Testament church was formed, the understanding of prophetic details was veiled. In Revelation

6:1, Christ is shown unsealing a book and revealing the events during the seven years of Tribulation.

(b) "Many shall run to and fro" (v.4). The end time would be characterized by excessive activity.

(c) "Knowledge shall increase" (v.4). The end time will be characterized by an explosion of worldly knowledge and information.

(3) An angelic oath for the end (vv. 5-10). When asked "How long?" the angel swears that it will be "time, times, and half a time," or that already familiar three-and-one-half-year period of the final "great tribulation" (Matt. 24:21, cf. Dan. 9-27, Rev. 13:5). This is paralleled in Revelation when there is a similar angel, here too lifting up his hands to heaven, similarly standing astride water and land, swearing there should be "delay no longer" (Rev. 10:6). The angel announces that the Tribulation events have at last arrived (Rev. 11-13). During this time Satan, through Antichrist, persecutes Israel and all those left on earth who will not wear the mark of the beast, which is 666 (Rev. 13:16-18). God commences to judge, destroy, and remove Satan's kingdom from the earth (Rev. 16:1, 2, 10).

(4) Days beyond the end (vv. 11, 12). Verse 11 speaks of thirty days beyond the 1,260 of the Great Tribulation (Rev. 12:6). Verse 12 attaches a blessing to the time of seventy-five days after the 1,260. Possibly these refer to the calendar of God's final judgments and rewards as Christ established His millennial reign on earth (Matt. 25:31-46). It may be that by seventy-five days after Armageddon and Christ's glorious coming, the millennial reign will at last be established in all of its prophesied perfections. Hence he that waits for this time is blessed.

(5) Abiding until the end (v.13). This is what Christ commanded Peter in John 21:22: "You follow Me." Everyone is called to serve God faithfully during all the days He has given, and find rest and peace in His service. Because Jesus died on the cross in their stead, all will "arise to your inheritance at the end of the days" (v.13; cf. 1 Cor 3:11-15).

Delegated Sovereignty (Daniel 4:1-37)

No king ever had a more prosperous or powerful kingdom than Nebuchadnezzar. His was the first and greatest of the four Gentile world empires (Dan. 2:31-45). Why? Because God, in His sovereign will, chose Nebuchadnezzar and exalted him to delegated autocracy. Then, in His sovereign grace, God humbled Nebuchadnezzar and brought him to repentance and faith in "the Most High [God]" (v.34). In the study of the fourth chapter, God, in His sovereign power, having stripped the mighty king of his delegated power, reestablished Nebuchadnezzar's authority with more greatness than before.

(1) **Nebuchadnezzar's confession of faith (vv. 1-3).** This chapter was written by Nebuchadnezzar after he came to know the Most High God as his personal Savior. He said, "I thought it good to declare the signs and wonders that the Most High God has worked for me" (v.2) He was ready to witness to the saving power of his sovereign Savior. The psalmist said, "Let the redeemed of the LORD say so" (Ps. 107:2).

The Most High God used Daniel, his Hebrew friends and their works as "signs and wonders" (v.2) to bring the mighty king to repentance. At conversion Nebuchadnezzar immediately recognized the sovereignty of God, saying, "His kingdom is an everlasting kingdom, and His dominion is from generation to generation" (v.3). After living with the beasts of the fields for seven years, and eating grass like cattle, he knew that no earthly monarch could be truly sovereign or everlasting. Now God did all of this to Nebuchadnezzar "that the living may know that the Most High [Sovereign] rules in the kingdom of men, and gives it [delegated rulership] to whomever He will, and sets over it the lowest of men" (v.17).

(2) Nebuchadnezzar's dream (vv. 4-18). In his dream he saw a large tree reaching to the sky. It was a tree of comfort, supplying fruit for the nations. This tree is a symbol of Nebuchadnezzar's delegated power. As he gazed, he saw an angelic "watcher, a holy one, coming down from heaven" (v.13), who commanded the great tree be chopped down.

(3) **Nebuchadnezzar's dream interpreted (vv. 19-27).** Daniel answered the king and said, "The tree that you saw . . . it is you, O king" (vv. 20, 22). The angelic watcher came down and said, "Chop down the tree and destroy it, but leave its stump and roots in the earth, bound with a band of iron and bronze" (v. 23). God would protect the stump of the great tree and restore it to power. Now Daniel pleaded with the king to "break off our sins" (v.27). But the king continued in his sins until God divested him of his delegated authority.

(4) Nebuchadnezzar stripped of his delegated power (vv. 28-33). One year later, while walking proudly in his palace (Prov. 16:18), he declared, "is not this great Babylon, that I have built for a royal dwelling by my mighty power and for the honor of my majesty?" (v.30)

Then the Most High God said from heaven, "King Nebuchadnezzar, to you it is spoken: the kingdom has departed from you" (v.31). Here is a great lesson. Our sovereign God gives, and He takes away. He exalts, and He humbles. The great difference between the power of man and the sovereignty of God is that man has no power to strip God of His sovereignty. "The LORD has established His throne in heaven, and His kingdom rules over all" (Ps. 103:19).

(5) Nebuchadnezzar's authority restored (vv. 34-36). When God restored Nebuchadnezzar to his kingship, the latter said, "I, Nebuchadnezzar, lifted my eyes to heaven . . . and I blessed the Most High and praised and honored Him who lives forever: For His dominion is an everlasting dominion, and His kingdom is from generation to generation" (v. 34). He recognized the sovereignty of God, and for the first time he understood the difference between absolute and delegated power.

(6) Nebuchadnezzar recognized the Sovereign God as his God. In essence he declared (v.37) that he, Nebuchadnezzar, would

(a)   praise the King of heaven;
(b)   extol the King of heaven;
(c)   honor the King of heaven;
(d)   declare that His works are truth;
(e)   declare that His ways are just;
(f)   known from experience that He is able to humble those who walk in pride, and strip them of all power, pride and worldly pretense.

Nebuchadnezzar declared that the Lord is Sovereign Ruler, the Most High God. {Daniel 5:1-31.}

The Fall of Babylon (Daniel 5:1-31)

Babylon was one of the most remarkable cities of the ancient world, famed for its architecture and, above all, for its hanging gardens.

(1) Babylon, the city. Babylon was built in a square, fifteen miles on each side, or a sixty-mile perimeter. Its wall was 350 feet high, 87 feet thick, with over two hundred lookout towers. The great Euphrates River flowed from north to south through the city, dividing Babylon into two sections. The banks of the river were walled with great bronze or brass gates at each of the avenues. There was a bridge at the central gate and ferry boats for all the other gates. The palace stood in the center of the city, with one section on each side of the river. It was connected by a subterranean passageway under the river, where large banquet rooms were located.

(2) Belshazzar's last feast. Even though besieged by the Medes and the Persians (Cyrus and his great army had besieged the city for many months), Belshazzar entertained the city of Babylon with festivity and drinking. He invited a thousand of his lords and princes, his wives and concubines, to a great feast (v.1), perhaps in one of the subterranean banquet rooms. Despite the siege by the Medes and Persians, the Babylonians believed that their city was impregnable. Little did they know that Cyrus had been working for months, changing the course of the great river so that it would bypass the city. On the night when they were feasting, drinking, and blaspheming the God of heaven, the river dried up, and Cyrus' army advanced down the riverbed (perhaps on both sides of the city). Careless in their drinking and partying the Babylonians left the gates open and the Medes and Persians took the city. It was prophesied a hundred years before Cyrus was born that he would take Babylon (Is. 44:28-45:5).

(3) Belshazzar's great sin. During the drunken orgy, Belshazzar "gave the command to bring the gold and silver vessels which his father Nebuchadnezzar had taken from the temple which had been in Jerusalem" (v.2). So far as we know, these sacred vessels had probably never been used until that night. When they were brought in, Belshazzar stood before the great banquet crowd and filled one of the vessels (perhaps a golden one) and "drank wine, and praised the gods of gold and silver, bronze and iron, wood and stone" (v.4). This was blasphemy-for those vessels had been sprinkled with blood and set apart for the worship of Jehovah God (Heb 9:21, 22).

(4) The handwriting on the wall. While they were drinking and blaspheming God, they saw that the "fingers of a man's hand appeared and wrote opposite the lampstand on the plaster of the wall of the king's palace" (v.5). The king was petrified with fear. His "countenance changed, and his thought troubled him, so that the joints of his hips were loosened and his knees knocked against each other" (v.6).

The wicked, ungodly king immediately sent for his wise men: "the astrologers, the Chaldeans, and the soothsayers" (v.7). But none of them could read the writing on the wall. Then the queen came in and said, "There is a man in your kingdom in whom is the Spirit of the Holy God. And in the days of your father, light and understanding and wisdom, like the wisdom of the gods, were found in him" (v.11). King Belshazzar summoned Daniel, saying, "Now if you can read the writing and make known to me its interpretation, you shall be clothed with purple and have a chain of gold around your neck, and shall be the third ruler in the kingdom" (v.16). Daniel said to the king, "Let your gifts be for yourself" (v.17), for he knew that the king would be dead before dawn. He was saying in effect, "The rewards I don't want, give them to somebody else." Then Daniel preached a great sermon to the wicked king (vv. 18-24): "This is the inscription that was written: MENE, MENE, TEKEL, UPHARSIN. This is the interpretation of each word: MENE: God has numbered your kingdom, and finished it; TEKEL: You have been weighed in the balances, and found wanting: PERES [the plural form of UPHARSIN]: Your kingdom has been divided, and given to the Medes and Persians" (vv. 25-28). This, then was a day of reckoning. Even though Daniel told the ungodly king that he did not want the rewards, the king proceeded to do what he had promised for Daniel (v.29). But before the sun rose over the city of Babylon, the Medes and the Persians had conquered it, slaying Belshazzar "and Darius the Mede received the kingdom" (vv. 30-31).

The Image of Gold (Daniel 3:1-30)

Chapter 3 introduces us to Nebuchadnezzar's image made of gold. He must have been influenced by Daniel's interpretation of his dream in chapter 2: "You are this head of gold" (Dan. 2:38). So Nebuchadnezzar built a great image of gold, a precious metal that does not deteriorate or tarnish, to immortalize himself.

(1) Nebuchadnezzar's golden image was ninety feet high and nine feet wide (v.1). If this seems out of proportion, remember that the image could have been much shorter if the pedestal were part of its measurement. Perhaps Nebuchadnezzar's image was dedicated to one of his favorite gods, or it may have been declared a new god. Either way, in the sight of God it was the folly of a self-centered king recalling the Pharaoh's

of Egypt, who built great pyramids to ensure their immortality. When the image of gold was completed, Nebuchadnezzar summoned all the dignitaries of his kingdom to the dedication. The image was erected outside Babylon, in the plain of Dura, where there would be nothing to distract from it (such as the magnificent hanging gardens and other architectural marvels). When all the guests were gathered before the image, Nebuchadnezzar directed his herald to declare the king's decree: at the sound of the music, they all were to fall down and worship the image-or be thrown into a fiery furnace(vv. 4-7).

(2) This was a real test of faith for the Hebrew nonconformists (vv. 8-22). They refused to bow down and worship the image. Knowing that they would not worship any god but Jehovah, the Chaldeans were watching them carefully. When they failed to bow down, the Chaldeans came to Nebuchadnezzar and accused the Jews. So the king summoned Shadrach, Meschah, and Abed-Nego Because they were very prominent in his kingdom, he gave them a second chance. He said, in effect, "we will play the music again, and this time you will fall down and worship the image, or be thrown into a fiery furnace." This was quite a test of their faith! The three Hebrews replied, "We have no need to answer you in this matter. If that is the case, our God whom we serve is able to deliver us from the burning fiery furnace and He will deliver us from your hand O king. But if not, let it be known to you, O king, that we do not serve your gods, nor will we worship the gold image which you have set up" (vv. 16-18). Their faith was not presumptuous. While they believed that God had the power to deliver them from the fiery furnace, they knew that could not demand it of God. They left it to His sovereign will. They did not have to talk it over; all three knew in their hearts they could not deny their God. Such was their great faith.

(3) Shadrach, Meshach, and Abed-Nego remind us of the remnant of the people of God who will endure all the fiery furnaces of the godless world, until their Messiah (the Lord Jesus Christ) comes back to the earth to usher them into the kingdom (Matt. 25:31-34). God speaks often of the remnant of Judah and Israel. The Scriptures record that

(a)   God saved a remnant of Judah after they were besieged by Assyrians for three years (Is. 37:1-4, 30-38, 2 Kin. 19:32-35.)

(b)   God has promised to save a remnant of the twelve tribes out of the Great Tribulation (Rev. 7:1-14).

(c)   God will bless the remnant of His people in the kingdom, and they will multiply and become innumerable (Zech. 8:12-17, cf. Matt. 25:31-34, Gen. 22:17, 18, Heb. 11:12, 13).

Now we all know how God delivered these three courageous Hebrew young people from the fiery furnace. More than just deliver them, He joined them in the fire and they fellowshipped together. The faith of Shadrach, Meshach, and Abed-Nego shone brighter and more lasting than Nebuchadnezzar's image of gold. For over two thousand years, there has been no trace of the golden statue; but the faith of Shadrach, Meshach and Abed-Nego shines as bright as the sun on a cloudless day.

The Tribulation Remnant (Daniel 6:1-28)

The Tribulation remnant consists of 144,000 members of the twelve tribes of Israel, who pledged by "the seal of the living God" to serve God during the Great Tribulation (Rev. 7:1-8). They will evangelize the nations and turn a countless multitude to Christ the Messiah. Jeremiah, the prophet, prophesied that in the end of the Times of the Gentiles, God could bring Israel and Judah out of all the nations of the world, back to their original homeland. God said, "For I am with you,' says the LORD, 'to save you; though I make a full end of all nations where I have scattered you, yet I will not make a complete end of you. But I will correct you in justice, and will not let you go altogether unpunished'" (Jer. 30:1-11). Even though Israel has been persecuted and scattered throughout the world, and without a homeland until 1948, God has never forsaken his chosen nation. For almost two thousand years they were a nation without a home; yet they have retained their national identity. When you see a Hebrew, you are looking upon a miracle. God did not make an end of all nations after the seventy years of captivity in Babylon; therefore, this prophecy is to be fulfilled in the future (Matt. 25:31-46). At this time of judgment of the nations, God will make an end of all the ungodly nations. The Jews' punishment will not be completed until the end of the seven years of Great Tribulation which are called "the time of Jacob's trouble" (Jer. 30:7). Israel's God will save 144,000 of the twelve tribes and seal on their foreheads the mark of ownership (Rev. 7:3). The 144,000 will not comprise the church: those of the church are not sealed on their foreheads; they are sealed with the Holy Spirit of promise (Eph. 1:13; 4:30) after having received the Lord Jesus Christ into their hearts as their personal Savior (Rom. 10:9, 10).

(1) Daniel's political prominence (vv. 1-3). This chapter ushers in the second Gentile world empire. After sixty-seven years the "head of gold" is replaced by the silver, and inferior kingdom (Dan. 5:30, 31). Daniel prophesied that the Medes and Persians would come and overthrow the Babylonian kingdom, and rule the known Gentile world.

(2) Daniel's jealous colleagues (vv. 4-9). Because King Darius favored Daniel over the other two presidents and all the princes, there was much jealousy; so they swore they would destroy Daniel, saying "We shall not find any charge against this Daniel unless we find it against him concerning the law of his God" (v.5). Now the presidents and princes had a voice in making laws for the Medes and Persians. When the laws were ratified by the king, no man could alter them. The difference between Nebuchadnezzar's kingdom and that of the Medes and Persians is simply that Nebuchadnezzar had total power. He was above all the laws of Babylon. But the Medo-Persian kings had to obey every statute. The law was the most powerful thing, more powerful than the king. Hence we have the phrase, "the law of the Medes and Persians, which does not alter" (v.8). After drafting a law that would destroy Daniel, these two presidents and princes met the king, flattering him and lying to him (vv. 6, 7).

(3) Daniel's prayer life (vv. 10, 11). The two presidents and princes knew that Daniel prayed to his God three times a day, at an open window facing Jerusalem. When Daniel heard the news, he went home. And in his upper room, with his windows open toward Jerusalem, he prayed (v.10), knowing that he could be cast into the den of lions, because "the law of the Medes and Persians does not alter." For Daniel valued prayer and his faith in God more than he valued his physical life. God has always preserved a remnant of Israel who value their faith in God more than they value their lives (Rom 11:1-5).

(4) Daniel's powerless king (vv. 12-18). When Daniel's enemies came before the king, citing evidence that Daniel had broken the law of the Medes and Persians, King Darius tried to save Daniel but ultimately had to obey the law. So he had Daniel thrown into the den of lions. "Now the king went to his palace and spent the night feasting; and no musicians were brought before him. Also his sleep went from him" (vv. 16, 18).

(5) Daniel's all-powerful God (vv. 19-23). What the king could not do, Daniel's God could do. He delivered Daniel from the lion's den, so

that "no injury whatever was found on him, because he believed in his God" (v.23).

(6) Daniel's enemies destroyed (v.24). The king commanded that these men who "framed" Daniel and who tried to destroy this great man of God, be cast "into the den of lions-them, their children, and their wives" (v.24). These wicked men, who would have destroyed Daniel, themselves suffered the fate which they had planned for God's prophet. So it will be, at the end of the Great Tribulation, when the nations of the world will be judged by God and destroyed, never to persecute God's people again (Rev. 19:11-21). The book of Esther dramatized this, when Haman conspired to hang Mordecai the Jew, whom he hated. Haman built a great gallows on which to hang Mordecai, but never got to use it. Actions taken against God, and against His perfect will for His people, are always frustrated at last. Instead of Mordecai hanging on the gallows, the king hanged Haman on Haman's own gallows (Esth. 7:10). This recalls the old axiom: "the chickens come home to roost." So they will, when all the ungodly nations that have persecuted the remnant of God's people for the past twenty-five hundred years are judged by God.

(7) Daniel's honor and prosperity (vv. 25-28). Now King Darius decreed "that in every dominion of my kingdom men must tremble and fear before the God of Daniel" (v.26). They were not to fear Daniel nor to tremble in his presence, but they were to respect and revere Daniel's God. Daniel was honored by the king, and he prospered in his kingdom because he was an upright, righteous, honest, God-fearing man. What a marvelous glorification of the Tribulation remnant, who "did not live their lives to the death" (Rev. 12:11).

The Vision of the Ram and Goat (Daniel 8:1-27)

About two years after his first vision (Dan. 7:1), Daniel experienced his second vision (v.1) during Belshazzar's third year as king of Babylon. His first vision had covered the four Gentile empires. His second vision covered the second and third empires (Medo-Persian and Greek). During the reign of these two empires, about 339 years, some of the most amazing prophecies in the Bible were fulfilled. Chronologically, chapters 7 and 8 occurred before Belshazzar's feast in chapter 5.

Daniel 1:1-23, because it was written in Hebrew, gave spiritual guidance and inspiration to the Hebrew captives. Daniel 2:4-7:28 was written in

Aramaic, the popular language of the day, perhaps so that some of the Gentiles might read it and come to know the God of heaven as Nebuchadnezzar did (in chapter 4). Daniel wrote a portion of his book in Hebrew (8:1-12:13), so the Hebrew people could know God's plan for their nation from the seventy years of captivity prophesied by Jeremiah (Jer. 25:11, 12), to the return of their Messiah, the Lord Jesus Christ, at the end of the Great Tribulation.

Daniel was in Babylon when he had this second vision but was transported in the vision to Shushan (or Susa), in the province of Elam, north of the head of the Persian Gulf (v.2). In a matter of moments, the God of heaven revealed to Daniel the future of Israel under the rule of the Medo-Persian and Greek empires for 339 years.

(1) In his vision he saw by the river of Ulai a ram with one horn higher than the other (vv. 3, 4). As he was pondering the vision, there appeared before him what looked like a man, even as a voice between the banks of the river was saying "Gabriel, make this man understand the vision" (vv. 15,16). Gabriel said to Daniel, "The ram which you saw, having the two horns-they are the kings of Media and Persia" (vv. 19, 20). Darius was the king of the Medes, and Cyrus (the stronger of the two) was the king of Persians. In this first year's reign, Cyrus had sent a written proclamation throughout his kingdom: All the kingdoms of the earth the LORD God of heaven has given me. And He has commanded me to build Him a house at Jerusalem which is Judah" (Ezra 1:2, cf. Ezra 6:1-3). Cyrus must have read Isaiah's prophecy where Jehovah God called him by name, saying, "He is My shepherd, and he shall perform all My pleasure, saying to Jerusalem, 'You shall be built,' and to the temple, 'Your foundation shall be laid'" (Is. 44:28).

Cyrus was called God's anointed for God had said, "I will go before you and make the crooked places straight; I will break in pieces the gates of bronze and cut the bars of iron" (Is. 45:1-7). God did all of this for the Jews who were captives in Babylon. Cyrus was chosen by God to bring about the Jews' return to Judea, and the rebuilding of the city of Jerusalem and the temple. Those who first returned (approximately 50,000) came under Zerubbabel and Jeshua (Ezra 2:64). Upon arriving in Jerusalem, they immediately built the altar for their morning and evening burnt offerings to God (Ezra 3:1-7). The Jews gradually rebuilt the city of Jerusalem, the walls, and the temple under Zerubbabel, Joshua, Ezra, Nehemiah, and Zechariah.

(2) The male goat from the west was Greece (vv. 5-8, 21. The words "without touching the ground" refer to the swiftness of the attack and conquest by the "notable horn," Alexander the Great (v.5). With foot soldiers and cavalry, Alexander conquered the Medo-Persian Empire in an unparalleled campaign (336-323 BC) of military conquest. The words "furious" (v.6) and "rage" (v.7) are the only adequate words to describe Alexander's implacable hatred of the Persians, who for two centuries had humiliated and trampled on the beauty of the cities of Greece. His conquest of Persia, Palestine, Babylon, Egypt, and Western India helped spread Greek culture and language everywhere, which is why the "good news" of the New Testament was later to be penned in Greek, the world language of the day.

(3) The Greek Empire split into four parts (v.8). Alexander the Great died suddenly at Babylon in 323 BC, at the age of thirty-three. Upon his death, Alexander's four generals (and then their heirs) became rulers of the conquered empire. These newly created Greek dynasties fought battle after battle to redivide the conquered land. The four horns represent these kings, and correspond to the four wings and four heads on the Greek leopard in the vision in Daniel 7:6. Palestine became a football to be fought over by the Greek kings of Syria and the Hellenistic kings of Egypt.

(4) Out of the Syrian-Greek horn was to come a persecutor of Judah (vv. 9-12). From the dynasty of the Hellenistic kings of Syria would arise Antiochus Epiphanes who persecuted Israel from 168-165 BC. He was the little horn of the Greek Empire as well as a type of the little horn of the revived Roman Empire . . . the Antichrist. He sought to erase the worship of the one true and living God from the earth;

(a)   He ordered the Sabbath day to be violated.

(b)   He sprinkled God's temple in Jerusalem with swine's blood.

(c)   He set up an idol of Jupiter in the temple

Over the next decade God used a pious, priestly family, the Maccabees (or "Hammers"), whose family name was Hasmon, to lead Israel to defeat huge Syrian armies. The temple was recovered, cleansed, and rededicated (165 BC). The security and freedom brought about by God through the Maccabees was maintained even when the Romans came in 63 BC, God always destroys the persecutors of Israel and brings their works to nothing.

The Vision of Seventy Weeks (Daniel 9:1-27)

This complex chapter is crucial to biblical prophecy. If we correctly interpret the seventy weeks (literally, seventy "heptads" or "sevens") that "are determined for your people and for your holy city" (v.24), we will better understand the things that will come to pass in the last days before the rapture of the church and the Great Tribulation. Most scholars translate "sevens" as periods of seven years, so seventy sevens would be 490 years. This would take us up to the coming of Christ; and the last week goes beyond, to the Tribulation.

It was through studying Daniel's Seventieth Week that Lepold Cohn, a Russian rabbi, realized that the time for the coming of the Messiah had already passed, and he concluded that the Messiah must have come by AD 70! Cohn sought advise from an older rabbi who told him that you could find anything in New York and to go to New York to find the Messiah. Cohn took the older rabbi quite literally, sold nearly all that he had to finance the journey to New York and there started his search for the Messiah. One day, as he was walking by a building he heard singing. Entering the hall, he heard the gospel being preached and later that day accepted Jesus as his Messiah. He then brought a stable, cleaned it out, procured folding chairs, and started holding gospel meetings of his own. Thus, from a literal understanding of this passage in Daniel was born the American Board of Missions to the Jews!

We must remember that all prophecy concerning Israel and the Messiah is linked to the period of "seventy sevens." Also we must allow Scripture to interpret Scripture (2Pet. 1:20, 21).

(1) In the first year Darius' reign as king of the Chaldeans, Daniel began to understand Jeremiah's prophecy about the seventy years of captivity (Jer. 25:11, 12).He noted the fact that for 490 years Israel had failed to keep even one sabbatical year for the land (Lev. 25:1-7). so that now their God was collecting the entire seventy years they owed (vv. 1, 2).

(2) Daniel felt deeply burdened by his concern for the future of his people and the city of Jerusalem.

In prayer he sought the mercy of God for Israel:
His prayer was bold—"I set my face toward the Lord God" (v.3).

(a)   His attitude was humble—"to make request by prayer and supplications, with fasting, sackcloth, and ashes" (v.3).

(b)   He confessed the greatness of God—"O Lord, great and awesome God, who keeps His covenant and mercy with those who love Him, and with those who keep His commandments" (v.4).

(c)   He confessed the sins of the nation Israel-We have sinned" (vv.4-16).

(d)   His plea—"Now therefore, our God, hear the prayer of Your servant" (vv. 17-19).

(3) The angel Gabriel interrupted Daniel's prayer and revealed to him Israel's future. Daniel wrote, "Yes while I was speaking in prayer, the man Gabriel, whom I had seen in the vision at the beginning, being caused to fly swiftly, reached me about the time of the evening offering. And he informed me . . .

(a)   'I have now come forth to give you skill to understand'; 'And I have come to tell you. "consider the matter, and understand the vision'" (vv. 21-23).

God wanted Daniel to know and understand the seventy sevens of years that he had determined for Israel and Jerusalem. Israel had lived through sixty-nine sevens of years, or 483 years, with but seven years remaining judged upon them and their city.

(4) "Seventy weeks are determined for your people and for your holy city" (v.24). The Hebrew word for week is shavua, which literally means "seven." But is this seven days or seven years? There is a clue in another chapter where Daniel said, "In those days I, Daniel, was mourning three full weeks"—or shavua, in the original (Dan. 10:2, 3). Here it means weeks of days, literally "three sevens of days."

If the seventy weeks were weeks of days, this would mean that the holy city and the walls would be rebuilt and destroyed again, and the Messiah would be "cut off," crucified (Matt. 27:35), and the six prophecies of Daniel (v.24) would all come to pass in 490 days-obviously impossible.

The Hebrew people had sevens of years as well as sevens of days. For example, when Jacob had served Laban seven years for his daughter Rachel, he was given Leah, the first born, and Laban said unto him, "Fulfill her week, and we will give you this one also for the service which you will serve with me still another seven years" (Gen 29:21-28). Here, one "week" is seven of years.

(5) The three periods of the seventy sevens of years:

(a)   The first period of seven sevens of years, or forty-none years, began "in the month of Nisan [April], in the twentieth year of King Artaxerxes"—445 BC (Neh. 2:1-8). Artaxerxes commissioned Nehemiah to rebuild Jerusalem and the walls (v.25). See Ezra, Nehemiah, and Zechariah.

The second period of sixty-two sevens of years, or 434 years plus forty-none years, totals 483 years with the Messiah (Christ) being cut off (crucified) in the month of Nisan (April) in AD 32. Allowing for Hebrew prophetic "years" of 360 days, this comes out to be exactly 483 years from the time Nehemiah was commissioned by King Artaxerxes to build the walled city. Actually, that Hebrew calculation dates back to the Flood. According to the book of Genesis, the Flood began in the six hundredth year of Noah's life, on the seventeenth day of the second month (Gen. 7:11); and the Flood came to an end on the seventeenth day of the seventh month (Gen 8:4). This was a period of five months of thirty days each, exactly 150 days (Gen. 7:4). This indicates that as far back as the Flood, a year was reckoned to be 360 days, not 365 days as we calculate (v.26).

(b)   The third period, the seventieth seven of years, or seven years plus 483 years, brings Israel down to the close of 490 years that Jehovah determined for the city and the Great Tribulation (Matt. 24:21, 22; Rev 7:13, 14).

In the synagogue at Nazareth our Lord read from Isaiah 61:1 and 2, ending with "the acceptable year of the LORD," detailing the blessing of His First Advent in grace to Israel. He told them, "Today this Scripture is fulfilled in your hearing" (Luke 4:16-21). The next line in Isaiah reads (but is not quoting Christ), "And the day of vengeance of our God." This is still in the future. Our Lord acknowledged the gap between His first and second comings, a gap surveyed in several Old Testament prophecies with comment.

Now there is similar gap between verses 26 and 27. The 69 sevens of years, or 483 years were fulfilled by the crucifixion of Christ. However, the seventieth seven, or the last seven years, are still in the future because there are six prophecies that must be fulfilled during the seventy sevens of years before the 490 years determined for Israel come completely to pass. Gabriel said to Daniel (v. 24), "Seventy weeks are determined for your people and for your holy city

> (a) "to finish the transgression"—the end of backsliding for the Hebrew nation, who will never again be apostate; this is yet future;
>
> (b) "to make an end of sins"—as a nation they will no longer make a practice of sinning; this is yet future;
>
> (c) "to make reconciliation for iniquity"—they will be reconciled to God by faith in the death, burial, and resurrection of Christ, their Messiah (Zech. 12:9-11; Rom. 11:25-27)-as a nation they will repent; this is yet future;
>
> (d) "to bring in everlasting righteousness"—this is God's righteous kingdom that Christ will Christ will establish on earth when He comes again (Heb. 1:8, 9, cf; Is. 9:6, 7 Rev. 19:11-16); this is yet future;
>
> (e) "to seal up the vision and prophecy"—there will be no more need for visions and prophecies for Israel, for all will have come to pass; this is yet future;
>
> (f) "to anoint the Most Holy"—or the Most Holy Place, the kingdom temple this is yet future;

The Messiah was "cut off" on Calvary over 1900 years ago. This means that the first 483 years of the seventy sevens are past; they were literally fulfilled in every detail. Doesn't it stand to reason that the seventieth seven will also have a literal fulfillment? The Great Tribulation is yet to be.

We know from history that between verses 26 and 27 the church age occurred. This was a mystery to the prophets; none of the writers of the Old Testament books possessed any foreknowledge of the New Testament church (Eph. 3:9, Col. 1:26, 27).

(6) The seventieth week—"Then he [the prince] shall confirm a covenant with many for one week"—or seven years (v.27). There are two princes mentioned in this chapter:

    (a)   "Messiah the Prince" (v.25).
    (b)   The prince that shall come—"the people of the prince who is to come shall destroy the city and the sanctuary" (v.26).

Christ the Messiah will not return to this earth until the end of the Tribulation (Rev. 19:11-21). The Roman army under Titus destroyed Jerusalem in AD 70. Therefore, the prince (v.26) who ratifies the covenant with the Jews for seven years will be a Roman-the little horn of Daniel (Dan 7:8). He is also "the man of sin" (2 Thess. 2:3, 4) and "a beast . . . out of the sea"—the sea being the ten kingdoms of the revived Roman Empire (Rev. 13:1-10). "In the middle of the week [seven years] he shall bring an end to sacrifice and offering. And on the wing of abominations shall be one who makes desolate" (v. 27; cf Matt. 24:15-22). He will stop the sacrificial offering and worship, and desecrate the Holy Place, the temple. However, before the seventieth week can come to pass.

    (a)   a remnant of Israel and Judah will return and possess the land of Israel in troublesome times (Jer. 30:1-24). In 1948 Israel became a nation; this could be the beginning of the end of the Times of the Gentiles (Luke 21:24).
    (b)   the temple will be rebuilt either before or during the first three-and-one-half years of the Tribulation. Unless the temple be rebuilt, the prophecy of the "abomination of desolation" (Matt. 24:15) spoken of by Daniel the prophet could not come to pass.

Daniel, the Prophet: His Visions

In the second six chapters of Daniel, we have what could be called "The Old Testament Book of Revelation" Here we discover vision after vision which God showed to Daniel, so that His people might have the security and stability of knowing, through dark times, that:

(1) Their God knows all that will come to pass;
(2) He has control of coming events;
(3) In the end His righteousness will triumph over evil.

The two Biblical prophets to whom God revealed the future most plainly were Daniel (in the Old Testament book of Daniel) and John (in the New Testament book of Revelation). Both men were described as being especially beloved of God. Daniel is called by the angel, "O man greatly beloved" (Dan. 10:19), and of John we read, "The other disciple whom Jesus loved" (John 20:2). Seeing these visions was a great privilege withheld from ordinary men, "but holy men of God spoke as they were moved by the Holy Spirit" (2 Pet. 1:21).

The visions appeared to Daniel between 606 BC, when Nebuchadnezzar conquered Jerusalem the first time, and 536 BC, which was the third year of Cyrus the Persian (Dan. 10:1), and the first year of Darius the Mede (Dan. 11:1). Why, then, do some critics date the book of Daniel in the second century BC, or more specifically, in 168 B.C? The answer is threefold:

(1) Some critics simply reject the idea from the start that God can enable men to prophesy the future in such accurate detail.
(2) Daniel 8:11 seems to be a reference to King Antiochus IV of Syria's desecration of the temple in Jerusalem in 168 BC
(3) Since this seems to be the last predicted item before the New Testament era, they date the book of Daniel at this time, 168 BC

There is evidence, however, that at least by the year 270 BC, when the Old Testament was translated into Greek in the Septuagint, that the book of Daniel was totally accepted as an unquestioned part of the Old Testament on the grounds of its having been written long before by Daniel, the prophet of God. Dead Sea Scroll manuscripts of Daniel show the book was revered and popular in the second century BC

Daniel 2:4-7:28 is written in Aramaic, a Semitic language related to Hebrew, quite possibly because Nebuchadnezzar, in one of his typical fits, ruled that during this period all writing would be in the leading world language of the day. Thus, as John wrote the New Testament book of Revelation with its many visions for God's people, in Greek, the common language of his day, so also Daniel wrote the Old Testament book of visions at least partially in the common language of Daniel's day, as a foretaste of what was to come.

The last six chapters contain so magnificent an array of visions that have already come true, that this section of the Bible alone proves that God indeed knows the future and has declared it to us through His servants the prophets.

The Vision of the Four Beasts
(Daniel 7:1-28)
The Vision of the Ram and Goat
(Daniel 8:1-27)
The Vision of the Seventy Weeks
(Daniel 9:1-27)
The Vision of the Angel in Linen
(Daniel 11:1-45)
The Vision of the Struggling Kings
(Daniel 11:1-45)
The Vision of the Angel's Oath
(Daniel 12:1-13)

The Times of the Gentiles (Daniel 2:1-49)

Nebuchadnezzar had a dream that troubled his spirit so much that he could not sleep (vv. 1-11). "Then the king gave the command to call the magicians, the astrologers, the sorcerers, and the Chaldeans to tell the king his dreams. So they came and stood before the king" (v.2). All claimed to have magical powers beyond the ordinary man. Astrologers claimed to know the future by divining the heavens. The Chaldeans claiming to have astrological powers were considered to be the priests of the Chaldean people. Isaiah warned Babylon of God's coming judgment, because they trusted in the astrologers. Isaiah said, "Let now the astrologers, the stargazers . . . save you from what [God's judgments] shall come upon you" (Is. 47:12-14) This stargazing cult has continued to grow throughout the world to this very day; and God still condemns it. The spiritualists claim power to communicate with the dead; they are known as mediums. This, too, is condemned by the Lord (1 Sam. 28:7-19).

(1) The dream disturbed the king and exposed the fraudulent wise men of Babylon (vv. 3-12). Nebuchadnezzar told them, "I have had a dream, and my spirit is anxious to know the dream" (v.3). The crafty Chaldeans said, "O king, live forever! Tell your servants the dream and we will give the interpretation" (v.4). King Nebuchadnezzar replied, "If you do not make the dream known to me, and its interpretation, you shall be cut in pieces" (v.5), going on to say, "Therefore tell me the dream, and I shall know that you can give me its interpretation" (v.9) The king's reasoning made sense-surely anyone who could foretell the future could also explain

the dream. But the wise men failed, and the king decreed they should all be put to death, including Daniel and his friends, who were not with the wise men when they appeared before Nebuchadnezzar.

(2) Daniel came to the rescue of the wise men, his three friends, and himself (vv. 13-25). Hearing the bad news, Daniel responded like a man of action in seven important ways:

   (a) He went to Arioch, the king's appointed executioner, asking, "Why is the decree from the king so urgent" (v.15), and requested to be taken before the king.

   (b) He went before the king and requested time so that he could learn the dream, and master its interpretation. This was an act of great faith.

   (c) He went to his three friends who had faith in the God of heaven, and the courage of their convictions.

   (d) He and his three friends addressed God in prayer.

   (e) When God revealed the dream and the interpretation to him in the night vision, Daniel blessed, praised, and exalted the God of heaven (vv. 19-23). Read these beautiful words of exaltation and praise to God for answered prayer. We should always thank God for every answer to prayers: we should thank Him before we get the answer.

   (f) He then went back to Arioch, who was under orders from the King to destroy all wise men in Babylon, and requested that he be brought again before the King.

   (g) Drawing power from God in heaven, he went before the king, ready to reveal the dream and the interpretation which God had made known to him "in a night vision" (v.19).

(3) Daniel made known to the king his dream and the interpretation (vv. 26-45). The king asked Daniel, "Are you able to make known to me the dream which I have seen, and its interpretation?" (v.26). Daniel seized the opportunity to witness for the God of heaven, but first he reminded the king that his wise men could not explain the meaning of his dream. Then Daniel said, "There is a God in heaven who reveals secrets, and He has made known to King Nebuchadnezzar what will be in the latter days" (v.28). Daniel gave God all the glory, saying, "But as for me, this secret has not been revealed to me because I have more wisdom than anyone living" (v.30). This was true humility.

(4) Now we come to the dream (vv. 31-35). In five short verses, God gave to the world a prophetic picture of the Times of the Gentiles (Luke 21:24), starting with the seventy years of Hebrew captivity in Babylon beginning in 606 BC, and continuing to the end of the Great Tribulation, when Christ (whom Nebuchadnezzar saw in his dreams as the stone "cut out without hands") would crush the Gentile world powers and establish His kingdom on this earth (Matt. 25:31-46). The stone "cut out without hands" does not portray the first coming of the Lord Jesus Christ, who emerged initially as "the Lamb of God who takes away the sins of the world" (John 1:29). But when Jesus comes the second time, it will be in power as great as that of the stone cut out without hands, and will grind the Gentile kingdoms to powder; He will rule and reign on the throne of His father David as "KING OF KINGS AND LORD OF LORDS' (Rev. 19:11-16).

(5) Daniel interpreted the dream (vv. 36-45). He said, "This is the dream. Now we will tell the interpretation of it before the king . . . you are this head of gold" (vv. 36-38). God had given this pagan king power over the earth, man and beast, making Nebuchadnezzar the greatest of all the world rulers. Fulfilling God's sovereign purpose, Nebuchadnezzar was summoned to punish Israel because they had forsaken their God in favor of false gods. The Lord said, "And now I have given all these lands into the hand of Nebuchadnezzar the king of Babylon, My servant" (Jer. 27:6).

God called Nebuchadnezzar, the heathen king, His servant. Why? Because Nebuchadnezzar, without knowing it, was doing the will of God. Nebuchadnezzar was fulfilling God's purpose. For God in His foreknowledge had predestined the salvation of this mighty king. "The Sovereignty of God and Salvation." God had ordained that Nebuchadnezzar would come to the place where he would place his faith in the Most High God, and humbly commit himself to the Lord. At that time in history, Babylon was the first of the four Gentile world powers.

After Daniel said of the great image, "You are this head of gold" (v.38) he added, "After you shall arise another kingdom inferior to yours"—on the part of the image that was silver (v.39). The latter kingdom was the Medo-Persian Empire that overthrew the Babylonians. The third kingdom (of brass) was the Greek Empire. The fourth and last of the great Gentile world powers was the Roman Empire (of iron). The ten toes of the image represent the ten kings that will be in power in the Great Tribulation, when Christ, the crushing stone, finally will fall on their feet and grind the entire Gentile world system into powder.

Following the four Gentile world empires, there will come a fifth-the kingdom of God on earth. The stone that is hewn without hands, the Lord Jesus Christ, will rule and reign on the throne of His father David for a thousand years. But at the end of that time, the kingdom of God will continue. Only then will there be a new heaven and a new earth (Rev. 21:1).

(6) When King Nebuchadnezzar heard the dream, and its analysis, he grew excited. "The king answered Daniel, and said, "Truly your God is the God of gods, the Lord of kings, and a revealer of secrets, since you could reveal this secret"" (v. 47). And what did Daniel do after Nebuchdnezzar honored him as a great man? He requested of the king that his three Hebrew friends be exalted with him, and the king complied.

When we give God the glory for our successes in life, then the kingdom of God has been spiritually set up in our hearts. Until Jesus comes, the Lord reigns in our lives. God is given His proper place, and we are given ours, which is under His rule. We need more Daniels serving God.

The Vision of the Four Beasts (Daniel 7:1-28)

The empires in Daniel's vision (chapter 7) are identical to the empires of Nebuchadnezzar's dream in chapter 2. The difference is that Nebuchadnezzar saw the four Gentile empires from man's standpoint: he saw only their human glory. Daniel saw them from God's viewpoint: corrupt and ruthless.

(1) Daniel's vision occurred in the first year of Belshazzar's reign over Babylon (about 553 BC). So chronologically, Daniel's vision in chapter 7 came before chapter 5, but the Holy Spirit inspired Daniel to insert it in the second half of the book of Daniel. The first half of Daniel (1-6) is historical and biographical and includes some generalized prophecy. Chapter 7-12 prophesy details covering the Times of the Gentiles from the Babylonian captivity to the seven years of the Great Tribulation in the future, which is called "the time of Jacob's trouble" (Jer. 30:7, cf. Rev. 7:14).

(2) Chapter 7 spans the Times of the Gentiles, from Nebuchadnezzar (606 BC) to the Antichrist (the little horn), who will come to power during

the Great Tribulation. Now let us compare Daniel's vision of the four great beasts with Nebuchadnezzar's dream of the image.

(a) "The first was like a lion" (v.4). This is the same as Nebuchadnezzar's head of gold (Dan. 2:37, 38)-the Babylonian Empire. Nebuchadnezzar was the one outstanding king of this first Gentile world empire.

(b) "A second, like a bear" (v.5). This is the same as the breast and arms of silver (Dan. 2:32, 39)-the Medo-Persian Empire. Cyrus was the outstanding king of this second Gentile world empire. Cyrus, a Gentile who did not know Jehovah God, was selected by the Lord over a hundred years before he was born. God anointed Cyrus to do His will, and to deliver Israel from the Babylonians and help rebuild their temple (Is. 44:28-45:4, cf. Ezra 1:14).

(c) "There was another, like a leopard" (v.6). This is the same as the belly and thighs of brass (Dan. 2:32-39)-the Greek Empire. Alexander the Great was the outstanding king of this third Gentile world empire.

(d) "I saw . . . a fourth beast" (v.7). The fourth beast in Daniel's vision was unlike any other-he was dreadful and exceedingly strong, with teeth of iron (vv. 7,8). He represents the same world power as the legs of iron and the feet of iron and clay (Dan. 2:40-43). The outstanding ruler (the Antichrist) of this empire is yet to appear. The ten horns in the head of the beast are the same as the ten toes of Nebuchadnezzar's image (Dan. 2:41-44). These ten horns or ten toes represent the ten kings who will lead the revived Roman Empire for over 650 years, longer than the other three empires combined. The second phase of the revived Roman Empire will last throughout the Great Tribulation. During this time, the little horn (Antichrist) will be in power. In the first half of the Tribulation he will befriend the Jews and confirm a covenant for seven years (Dan. 9:27). During the last half of the Tribulation he will be empowered by Satan (v. 25; cf. Rev. 13:2). He will dethrone three of the kings (v.8). The other seven will become puppets (v.20). The book of Revelation details the satanic powers he will exert during the three-and-one-half year reign (Rev. 13: 1-8). He will possess all the characteristics of Satan (Rev. 13:2). In the days of the ten kings with the little horn (the Antichrist), Christ will come and establish the kingdom of God upon earth (vv. 13, 22; cf. Dan. 2:34, 35, 44, 45; Luke 1:31-33; Rev. 11:15). When Christ comes, He will sit upon the throne of His human ancestor, King David (Is. 9:6, 7), and will rule in eternal righteousness. (Heb. 1:8, 9).

The Vision of the Struggling Kings (Daniel 11:1-45)

This chapter is as detailed and complex as any in the entire Bible. Once we admit that Almighty God does indeed reveal the future, we begin to appreciate and accept the wondrous detail and specific prophecies in this chapter as an outflowing of His omnipotence and omniscience. Knowing the future, He assures its certainty. Christ testified that the book of Daniel is inspired, genuine, and true (Matt. 24:15) because it is from God. Let us review this chapter's content and direction:

(1) Verse 2. The four great and powerful rulers of Persia were Cyrus, Ahasuerus (Cambyses), Darius Hystapes, and Xerxes. Malachi, the last Old Testament author, ended the Old Testament canon in 420 BC During this intertestamental period (420-4BC) the Jews were living in the far-flung Persian world.

(2) Verse 3, 4, Alexander the Great of Greece, at twenty years of age, inherited the Macedonian armies of his assassinated father, Philip II, and united the Greek city-states to the south by threat of annihilation. In thirteen years (336-323 BC) he conquered the western world. At his early death in Babylon, his conquered world split into four warring quarters which pitted Hellenistic general-kings against one another for the next 150 years (Dan. 7:6; cf. 8:21, 22).

(3) Verse 5-12. Two of these kingdoms, Syria and Egypt, continually fought over Israel (323-200 BC), which lay as the prize between them. Syria was "the king of the North" and Egypt "the king of the South." The king's daughter (v.6)was Bernice, daughter of Ptolemy II, the Greek ruler of Egypt, who had married Antiochus Theous of Syria. Bernice was poisoned by him. Verses 7-9 speak of her brother, Ptolemy Energetes of Egypt. Verse 11 tells of Ptolemy Philopater of Egypt, victorious over and possessor of Palestine; verse 12 bemoans his later licentious life.

(4) Verse 13-20. Antiochus III (reigning 200-187 BC), greatest of Greek-Syrian kings, is mentioned in verse 13-19. While attempting to conquer Egypt, he recaptured Palestine for Syria at the Battle of Panias (198 BC). Verse 17 describes his futile attempt at marrying into Egypt through his daughter, Cleopatra (not the famous Cleopatra, queen of Egypt 150 years later). Verse 18 and 19 predict Antiochus' battle with the Romans as well as his death. Verse 20 foreshadows his short-lived follower, Seleucus Philopater (reigning 187-176 BC), who imposed taxes.

(5) Verse 21-30. Antiochus IV, the Greek ruler of Syria, was also called Epiphanes, meaning "illustrious," but because of his evil ways, he was notorious as Epimanes, or "maniac." Verses 21 and 23 call him vile and his reign deceitful. Verses 25-29 recount how the Romans, fearing Syria would become a rival to their fast-rising empire, in 168 BC, forbade him to enlarge his kingdom (v.30).

(6) Verse 30-35. When the Romans checked Antiochus' plan to attack Egypt, in rage he unleashed his army upon Jerusalem, which he hated because of the Jews' rejection of the Greek Jupiter cult. Verse 31 describes how he polluted the holy temple by sprinkling it with the blood of a pig (ceremonially unclean animal), and erecting within it a statue of Jupiter. The non-canonical, intertestamental (apocryphal) book of 1 Maccabees describes the revolt of the pious Jews, 168-165 BC, under the courageous and consecrated leadership of Judas the Maccabee ("Hammer"). Relying on God's strength and name, Judas "turned to fight the armies of the aliens" (Heb. 11:34). The Hebrew feast of Hanukkah celebrates the recapture and rededication of the temple in Jerusalem in the month of Kislev (December), 165 BC, and the consequent burning of the olive oil lamps for eight days (John 10:22, 23).

Note: Verse 31 and Daniel 9:27 place this abomination of desolation in the future. Christ, two hundred years later in AD 32, spoke of this "abomination of desolation" (Matt. 24:15). Thus He showed that the abomination by Antiochus was to be taken as a foreshadowing of the public blasphemy yet to be committed by the Antichrist in the middle of the seven years of Tribulation (Dan. 9-27). This would identify the Antichrist to those on earth at the time, and would launch the beginning of the final half of the seven years of "the Great Tribulation," stopped at last by Christ's return, in glory, at Armageddon (Matt. 24:15, 21, 31). Paul also confirmed this event (2 Thess. 2:3, 4). The theory that the Roman general Titus committed this abomination in AD 70 does not fit the history of those events. Titus did not desecrate the temple (his soldiers burned it against his orders); he never blasphemed God in it as Paul describes in 2 Thessalonians 2:3, 4. There was no opportunity for flight after the temple was captured. Matthew 24:15-18. The "tribulation" of the Jews in AD 70 chiefly took place before, not after, the seizure of the temple, as would have been required by Matthew 24:15-21. Furthermore, Christ did not come again "immediately after the tribulation of those days" (Matt. 24:29). The abomination of desolation lies ahead, and Middle East events point to its imminence. When it occurs it will again be like that of Antiochus IV who is the prototype of the Antichrist-the little horn of Daniel 7:7, 8 and the Beast "out of the sea" in Revelation 13:1-10.

(7) Verse 36-45. Scenes in the Scriptures sometimes shift from one location immediately in view to one in a distant vista. For example, Isaiah 14:4-7 addresses the king of Babylon, then shifts to Satan who stands behind him. In Ezekiel 28:2 the king of Tyre is the subject, but in verses 12-19 the shift is to Satan behind the king. So it is here: verse 36 shifts us to the satanic Antichrist, who is so much like Antiochus Epiphanes, and more. The Antichrist is here described in terms similar to the "little horn" of Daniel 7:8, 24,25; the "man of sin" of 2 Thessalonians 2:3, 4; and the "beast" of Revelation 13 who will reign supreme over all nations. "He was given authority to continue forty-two months" (Rev. 13:5). Today it is frequently speculated that he will be the ruler of the west (Rome revived-a confederated Europe); that the "king of the South" (v.40) will rule the now-confederated Arab nations; that the "king of the North" (vv. 40, 44) is the head of the Union of Soviet Socialist Republics; and that "the East" (v.44) is a confederation led by China. The events will happen in God's own time (Matt. 24:36, Acts 1:7), and he, the Antichrist, will at last be destroyed (v.45) at Armageddon (Rev. 16:16, cf. Rev. 19:11-21).

The Second Book of Chronicles

AUTHORSHIP

Jewish tradition has always assigned the authorship of 1 and 2 Chronicles to Ezra. This is strongly confirmed by two points of evidence: (1) The style of the books of Ezra and Chronicles are so similar that critics agree they must have been written by the same person. (2) The last two verses of 2nd Chronicles are repeated in the beginning of Ezra.

CONTEXT

At the time when this book was written, the people of Israel had reached a new crisis in their national history. When Ezra returned to Judea in 458 BC, the monarchy had been in abeyance for 130 years. Nearly eighty years had passed since the first of those who returned from captivity had begun to reestablish the nation in Jerusalem, but they and their descendants had accepted their position as subjects of the Persian government, and their civil government was on the same footing as that of a conquered people. It was for such an altered condition of the Hebrew people that Ezra rewrote the later history of their race.

HOW 2 nd CHRONICLES FITS INTO THE BIBLE

The author records events of the same period as that covered by the books of Samuel and Kings, and sometimes uses the same language; and so his work is properly placed where it is in the English Bible. However, he writes from a different standpoint and his work has a distinct character of its own.

SUMMARY STATEMENT

In 2 nd Chronicles, God places before the Jews such an aspect of their past history as would strengthen the religious element of their nationality and teach them that their highest glory is the special sovereignty of God over them.

HOW 2 nd CHRONICLES FITS TOGETHER

2nd Chronicles divides into two parts, recording the history of Solomon in chapter 1-9 and the history of the Judahite kings in chapters 10-36. It closes with the edict of Cyrus.

The most effective teaching is by repetition. God is trying, again and again to remind the nation of Israel of their heritage, where they had been and where they could be. A strong appeal for national return to God is given in 7:14—"If my people who are called by My name will humble themselves, and pray and seek My face, and turn from their wicked ways, then I will hear from heaven, and will forgive their sins and heal their land."

The Book of Amos

Amos is one of the most exciting and forward-looking books in the Bible. It is God's printout for today's happenings to a people called Israel.

AUTHORSHIP

The author, whose name comes from a Hebrew verb meaning "to carry a burden," by his own confession was "no prophet, nor was I the Song of a prophet" (7:14), but in his case God bypassed the professionals to enlist a sheep breeder and a gatherer of fruit from the sycamore tree. His hometown was Tekoa in the desert, twelve miles south of Jerusalem and six miles south of Bethlehem, overlooking the Dead Sea. Here he was occupied with managing sheep and pinching the fruit in such a way that it might grow and ripen properly as food for the poor.

CONTEXT

Often the people God uses are those who have a period of solitude in a desert place with Him. Think of God's theological college for Moses-the backside of the desert; Abraham-in the wilderness of Hebron; David-in the fields with his sheep, and later in the wilderness running from King Saul; Paul-three years in the Arabian desert; and Amos, from the wild wilderness to Bethel, the capital of the northern kingdom of Israel, where Jeroboam I had erected one of his golden calves for idolatrous worship. It was during the reign of Jeroboam II in the eighth century BC that the prophet from Tekoa opened an exciting portion of God's eternal drama. The stage is set for us to see in this small book God's zeal for righteousness and the eternal hope that He gives.

SUMMARY STATEMENT—

Amos, a Southerner from Judah, calls the idolatrous Northerners, Israel, to repent of their violence and social injustice and serve the Lord in righteousness.

HOW AMOS FITS TOGETHER AND KEY VERSE—

The seed of God's eternal purpose for the Jewish nation and their land is germinated in this revealing and remarkable book of nine chapters, which shows how today's struggles become tomorrow's triumphs. The book may be divided into four main parts, all of which are highlighted by the key verse, 4:12—"Therefore thus will I do to you, O Israel; because I will do this to you, prepare to meet your God, O Israel!"

(1) Prior to this verse, we see the patience of God in punishment. Chapters 1 and 2 proclaim God's judgment on the nations, and include indictments against Syria, Philistia, Phoenicia, Edom, Ammon, Moab, and Judah, finally focusing on Israel itself. The almighty and righteous God has not acted immediately by punishing the sinners, but finally His patience has been exhausted and to each nation He says, "I will send a fire" upon you!

(2) Chapters 3-6 are three sermons on the doom of Israel. The first announces coming judgment on Israel's present sins (ch. 3); the second denounces Israel's past depravity in failing to accept God's correction (4), and the third contains a lamentation for Israel's sin and doom, a call to repentance, and warnings concerning the coming of the Lord (5-6).

(3) The curtain now rises on the final act in this drama of God with a fivefold vision of His judgment in chapters 7-9. God illustrates His will through the figures of locust (7:1-3); a devouring fire (7:4-6); a plumb line (7:7-9); and a basket of summer fruit, ripe as Israel was ripe for judgment (8:1-14); and finally Amos sees the Lord Himself announcing the destruction of Israel (9:1-10). This section also contains a parenthetical account in which Amaziah the priest complains against Amos (7:10-17).

(4) After these messages of ruin and calamity, Amos ends his prophecy with the promise of Israel's restoration (9:11-15). God is almighty and thorough in His judgment, but He is also the same in His mercy. With this bright promise, He brings to a conclusion His eternal and triumphant drama.

The First Epistle of Paul
The Apostle to The Corinthians

AUTHORSHIP

The book of 1 Corinthians was written by the apostle Paul to a church that he had founded in the early part of his ministry. The Pauline authorship of the letter is scarcely doubted by anyone. Vocabulary, contents, and style all point to Paul. 1 Corinthians is also the first book to be credited specifically to Paul in the works of Clement of Rome (about AD 95).

HOW 1 CORINTHIANS FITS INTO THE BIBLE

This is a long, varied, and extremely important epistle. Because it deals with a church coming out of the darkness of paganism, it is most helpful even today. However, the church problems of Corinth also sound strangely familiar when one sees the things going on in many churches of the Western world today. Another benefit of this book is that it is so utterly practical and relates to common problems and real people in a very special way.

HOW 1 CORINTHIANS FITS TOGETHER

Because Paul is answering several questions asked by the Corinthians as well as commenting on other problems that he had heard about through "those of Chloe's household," a more detailed outline is needed than in some of the simpler epistles:

(1) Divisions in the Church (chs. 1-4)
(2) Immorality in the Church (ch. 5)
(3) The Law Courts and the Church (ch. 6)
(4) Christian Marriage (ch. 7)
(5) On Meat Offered to Idols (chs. 8-10)
(6) Head Coverings and the Lord's Supper (ch. 11)
(7) Spiritual Gifts in the Church (chs. 12-14)
(8) The Doctrine of Resurrection (ch. 15)
(9) The Collection and Personal Notes (ch. 16)

The Corinthian believers were richly blessed with spiritual gifts that would outfit this body of Christians to carry out the Great Commission, but because of immaturity, carnality, and lack of spiritual growth they were unable to accomplish God's will. There was internal confusion, strife, and division. Their immaturity and carnality produced the following problems:

They were following human leadership instead of God.
They were admiring human wisdom.
They were judgmental of each other.
They questioned authority.
They permitted immorality in the church.
Some were taking each other into the world's courts.
They were not yielding the physical body to the Lord's service.
They were confusing the marriage obligations.
They were misusing their liberty in Christ.
Some had become stumbling blocks to other believers.
They were making no financial provision for Paul and were taking his service for granted.
They were grumbling and complaining.
They were selfish and greedy.
Some were misusing the elements of the Lord's Supper and violating its order.
They were magnifying the "showy" gifts of the Spirit and minimizing the others.
They were guilty of not loving.
They were misusing the gift of tongues.
Some were questioning the resurrection of Christ.
They were unfaithful in their regular giving.

Paul wrote this epistle to correct such problems within the church, and in each chapter you will read his stern rebuke and positive redirection. He admonished his readers to correct these things in the light of the judgment of Christ and the examining of their works (1 Cor. 3:11-15). His lessons need to be learned and applied, not just in the first century but also in the twenty-first century.

The Book of Ezra

Ezra is named after the man who exercised a significant influence on the history of Israel between the years 536-458 BC. His book was the revelation of God at this time in Israel's experience.

The importance of the book of Ezra is inestimable. It provides us with the only information available regarding the historical period immediately following the exile. Ezra chronicles the day-by-day events of those epochal times.

AUTHORSHIP

The book does not give the name of the author but the last four chapters (7-10) were clearly Ezra. Here he speaks in the first person. This suggests the likelihood that he wrote the whole book.

The name EZRA means "Help" in Hebrew. He was the faithful scribe and priest, descended from Hikiah the high priest in the reign of Josiah. The only Biblical record concerning Ezra is found in the last chapters of this book and from Nehemiah 8 and 12. Here we learn that Ezra was a priest of great piety and learning who lived in Babylon during the reign of Artaxerxes.

HOW EZRA FITS INTO THE BIBLE

The book is strategic because it perpetuates the scarlet thread of redemption found in the Holy Scriptures, by continuing the genealogical record of the seed of the woman (Gen. 3:15). The book registers the names of the families of Israel who returned from exile in Babylon. Those whose genealogy could not be established were rejected. Thus the purity of the race was maintained.

The book records the return of God's people to Jerusalem under the protecting hand of the Almighty. It was by the will of God that they had been taken captive to Babylon, as shown in the books of Kings and Chronicles. God had not abandoned His people, indeed, as the books of Ezekiel and Daniel demonstrate. He was continually watching over them. And now, by His sovereign will they were coming home. The reader will be inspired by this account to practice the presence of God and depend on Him alone for protection and provision of every need.

KEY VERSE: 6:14b

"And they built and finished it, according to the commandment of the God of Israel, and according to the command of Cyrus, Darius, and Artaxerxes, king of Persia."

HOW EZRA FITS TOGETHER

The book falls naturally into three parts: (1) The return of the Exiles under Zerubbabel (1-2), (2) The Restoration of the Worship of the LORD (3-6), and (3) The Return of the Exiles under Ezra (7-10).

Besides recounting the Israelites' return to their land, the book also records the religious reformation among those who had departed from observing the divine ordinances following the death of their leaders, Zerubbabel and Joshua. There was a clarion call to repentance and renunciation of foreign wives and their idolatrous practices. The sorrow the Israelites expressed for sin reveals hearts broken before God. The penitential prayer that followed is beautiful. It could be a model prayer for confession of sin. The book closes with a list of those who had married foreign wives.

In conclusion, the book magnifies respect for the Word of God. It brings into focus the law of the Lord as the rule of human conduct and relationships to God and man. Reestablishment of the Mosaic institutions, ordinances, and feasts reminded them of the great redemption of God's people and strengthened their faith. The purpose of the book is crystal clear: that Israel might be nourished in the words of faith and good doctrine. It is a book of repentance, revival, restoration, and renewal of faith and confidence of Israel in her great redemptive God.

The Book of Judges

Judges is a historical book of the Old Testament following the book of Joshua. The book presents a series of spiritual relapses into idolatry and ungodly living. It pictures man's weaknesses and God's strength. The judgment of God on His own people is a vital truth in this book, centering on spiritual failure and deliverance.

Judges receives its name from the Hebrew word Shophetim (the Hebrew name of the book), which designates the leaders who delivered Israel from foreign oppressors between the death of Joshua and the beginning of the monarchy (under King Saul). The root meaning of Shophetim is "to govern" or "to judge"; the "judges" were various "deliverers" or "saviors" who championed their people in times of crisis.

CONTEXT

The book covers the first 350 years of Israel's history in the land of Canaan. A strong centralized government had not yet arisen in Israel. The tribes were disorganized and weak. The statement is twice repeated that "in those days there was no king in Israel; everyone did what was right in his own eyes" (17:6; 21:25). It was a time of chaos and anarchy, when God's people often fell into sin and were judged for their idolatry and immorality, until a "judge" arose to champion their cause.

AUTHORSHIP

Jewish tradition attributes authorship of this book to Samuel. It is evident that this book manifests a unity of thought, and therefore was probably written and arranged by one person. And what could be more probable than that Samuel, who links the two periods of the judges and the kings, should have had a large hand in the writing of the book? The book nowhere names its author, however, and scholars disagree on this question.

THE CYCLE OF REPRESSION

Perhaps the most striking fact about this book is the recurring cycle of sin, suffering, supplication, and salvation that occurs in its pages. For a brief period the people of Israel enjoy a time of peace and prosperity. Instead of glorifying God for His blessings, however, the people fall into the double sin of idolatry and immorality-adopting the worship and pagan life-style of the heathen people in their midst. God's judgment then falls upon the disobedient and rebellious people (3:8, 12; 4:2; 6:1; 10:7; 13:1), who are subjugated by their enemies. Out of the depths of oppression Israel cries to God in repentance, and God sends a judge to free them from bondage, restoring peace and prosperity to the land. Alas, the people again become complacent and self-willed and the vicious cycle of sin-suffering-supplication-salvation is repeated.

HOW JUDGES FITS TOGETHER

The book is divided into three periods:

(1) The period immediately after the death of Joshua (1:1-2:5)
(2) The period of the judges (2:6-16:31) Twelve judges are listed: Othniel, Ehud, Shamgar, Deborah (with Barak), Gideon, Tola, Jair, Jephthah, Ibzan, Elon, Abdon, and Samson. Of these, six stand out preeminently: Othniel (3:7-11), Ehud (3:12-30), Deborah (4:1-5:31), Gideon (6:11-8:35), Jephthah (11:1-12:7), and Samson (13:1-16:31). These judges were only temporary "saviors"; they were able to deliver their people temporarily from oppression, but the final, once-and-for-all deliverance of God's people awaited the one and only Savior, our Lord Jesus Christ.
(3) The period of confusion and anarchy (17:1-21:25)

The book of Proverbs says, "Righteousness exalts a nation, but sin is a reproach to any people" (Prov. 14:34). This is perhaps the key message of the book of Judges. Without fear (reverence) of the Lord and a faithful keeping of His holy commandments, people become slaves of a vicious cycle of futility and lose the freedom intended for them-the glorious liberty of the children of God. When everyone does what is right in his own eyes, refusing to serve God, the true King of Israel, the way is laid open for confusion, chaos, collapse, and terrible misery.

The Book of Joel

Like a burst of sunlight on a darkened world, the apocalyptic book of Joel had its impact on his time and culture. It later helped to vitalize the apostle Peter's sermon at Pentecost about the living Messiah (Acts 2:16-21) and Paul's exposition of the unfathomable grace of God in the gospel (Rom. 10:13). It remains undimmed through the years in the darkness of our hedonistic society.

AUTHORSHIP

We know very little about Joel, the prophet who wrote this little book, either of his life or of the period of his prophecy. Perhaps the mystery is part of what makes Joel so constantly contemporary. The name Joel means "Jehovah is God," which may indicate the religious faith of his father Pethuel and his mother. There are thirteen other men named Joel in the Old Testament, but none of them can be identified with this prophet.

SUMMARY STATEMENT

Using a devastating plague of locusts as an illustration, Joel teaches that the day of the Lord-the time when He will reveal Himself in the destruction of His enemies and the exaltation of His friends-is surely coming.

HOW JOEL FITS INTO THE BIBLE

Joel is the second of the twelve so-called Minor Prophets, which in the Hebrew text constitute one book called "The Twelve." While Joel is a very short book, its prediction of the worldwide outpouring of the Holy Spirit is most important.

HOW JOEL FITS TOGETHER

The three chapters of Joel fall into two main parts: (1) The day of the Lord is heralded through the description of a plague of locusts (1:2-2:17); and (2) judgment is averted and blessings are bestowed (2:18-3:21).

KEY VERSE

The best single verse to characterize Joel from a positive viewpoint is 2:32a, which Paul quotes in Romans—"And it shall come to pass that whoever calls on the name of the Lord shall be saved." The most famous passage is 2:28-32, quoted by Peter in his Pentecost sermon.

The Book of Hosea

Hosea is the first of the so-called Minor Prophets. They are so called because of the size of the books and not because of their content. The name Hosea means "salvation," and is closely related to the name Joshua (which in turn is identical with the name of our Savior, Jesus). Hosea's name fits his task well, for he was the last prophet to Israel before that kingdom fell in 722 BC. He pleaded for his people to turn to God and be saved.

AUTHORSHIP

All that we know about the prophet is discovered from the autobiographical sections of the book itself. Hosea probably saw the ten tribes of his beloved Israel dragged away from the land which they had shamefully defiled by idolatry and immorality, into that exile and dispersion among the nations from which, even yet, they have not been re-gathered.

Hosea was a prophet to the northern kingdom, as the content of the book reveals. He was a contemporary with Amos, another prophet to Israel, and also with Micah and Isaiah, prophets to Judah. His ministry extended over half a century, and he lived to see the fulfillment of his prophecy in the captivity of Israel.

CONTEXT

Hosea may be called the prophet of the decline and fall of the northern kingdom. He sought to call the sinful and estranged nation back to God. He was the prophet of Israel's zero hour. The prophet stood midway in time between Moses and Christ, and began to prophesy two hundred years after the division of the united kingdom. His ministry included the last years of the northern kingdom. Most of his prophetic ministry evidently took place from 750 to 725 BC.

HOW HOSEA FITS TOGETHER

The book of Hosea may be divided into three major parts, as follows: (1) The Prophet's Married Life (Chs. 1-3); (2) Israel's Unfaithfulness to Yahweh and Consequent Judgment (Chs. 4-13); and (3) Israel's Conversion and Renewal: The Call to Repentance and the Promise of Forgiveness (Ch. 14).

Hosea married a woman named Gomer, who bore him two sons and a daughter. Afterward, she became a harlot and left home. Hosea's heart was broken beyond description. But God commanded Hosea to take the unfaithful harlot back into his home and to love her again. Out of this experience, Hosea grasped with rare insight the pain that is in the heart of God when His people forsake Him and sin against Him. Through the heartbreaking experience of his tragic marriage, the prophet had come to see Israel's sin against God in its deepest and most awful significance.

Beginning with chapter four, the private life of Hosea fades into the background and the emphasis is upon the Lord and Israel. The theme is the unfaithful nation and her faithful Lord. The book emphasizes the shame of sin, the fruit of backsliding, the love of the Lord for His wayward people, and the conditions of their restoration. The language of the book is plain and frank. Hosea's message is needed in our day when sin is glossed over and soft words are substituted for hard facts.

The Epistle of Paul
The Apostle to The Galatians

AUTHORSHIP

Paul wrote Galatians to stem the wave of criticism begun by a team of Judaizers who dogged Paul's steps as he planted churches throughout Galatia. These false teachers, whose aim was to convince Paul's Gentile converts to adhere to the Mosaic law, spread two rumors about Paul: first, that he was not an apostle; second, that he did not preach the gospel.

HOW GALATIANS FITS TOGETHER

A simple outline of the book divides it by Paul's answer to the charges: (1) "I am an apostle" (Chs. 1, 2) and (2) "I do preach the gospel" (Chs. 3, 6).

A slightly more detailed outline divides the book into three sections of two chapters each: (1) Personal: Paul defends his gospel (Chs. 1, 2); (2) Doctrinal: Paul refutes the legalistic Judaizers (Chs. 3, 4); (3) Hortatory: Paul exhorts the Galatians to live in Christian freedom and spirituality (Chs. 5, 6).

HOW GALATIANS FITS INTO THE BIBLE

Galatians is one of the earliest epistles of Paul, if not the earliest, and many have seen it as a sort of Romans in germ form. Galatians is a more emotional and brief treatment of the same topics handled in Romans; or we could say that Romans is a more developed and logical presentation of the message of Galatians. The great reformer Martin Luther was freed from his legalistic bondage through Romans and Galatians, and wrote a famous commentary on the latter. He even referred to Galatians as "my Katie von Bora," which was his beloved wife's name-high praise indeed, for both the woman and the book!

In spite of the fact that Galatians is a short book, it contains brilliant theological definition, classical development of thought, and able evangelical urgency. In it Paul clarifies the meaning of apostleship (1:), faithful proclamation (1:8-10) the nature of revelation (1:11-12), personal testimony (1:13-24), the relation of the law to grace, the sinner's identity with Christ's crucifixion (2:20), the Spirit's role in the believer's continuation in the faith (3:1-5), the nature of righteousness (3:6-9), the teaching that brought the Reformation to the world (3:9-11), the connection between Abraham's faith and Christ's imputation of righteousness (3:12-18), how the Old Testament believer is saved (3:19-26), the universal, trans-racial nature of Christ (3:27-28), the Christian as the inheritor of all the promises to Abraham (3:29), the nature of redemption and adoption (4:1-7), the bondage of reverting to the law as a basis for salvation (4:8-20), the bondage of legalistic living and the freedom of living under grace (4:21-31), law-based salvation as impossible and far below salvation founded on grace (5:1-4), the works of the flesh and the fruit of the Spirit (5:16-26), the practical expression of the fruit of the Spirit (6:1-6), sowing and reaping (6:7-10) and glorying in the Cross (6:11-17).

Perhaps no book, with the exception of Romans, covers the theological spectrum in so few words.

Galatians is the ringing of the Liberty Bell to all who are enslaved by sin.

The First Epistle of John

The First Epistle of John is one of the latest Biblical writings given to us by the Spirit of God. The epistle is not addressed to any particular church, but is thought of as a "circular letter" sent to several churches. It is a family epistle or letter-and may be designated as "the joy book" or "salvation letter." The epistle is a letter of fellowship, and can be rightly called a family letter because the believers are viewed as the family of God. This is attested to by the repeated use of the word children.

KEY WORDS: know, believe, love, and fellowship

AUTHORSHIP

The apostle John was probably the only one of the twelve apostles who did not suffer a martyr's death. After his imprisonment on the island of Patmos, his last years were spent in Ephesus, where he died and was buried. It would be supposed, then, that the epistle was written there in about AD 90.

The epistle is addressed to the believers or "born ones," so that they might distinguish between truth and error that was creeping into the churches of that day.

HOW 1st JOHN FITS INTO THE BIBLE

1st John is one of the most profound and spiritual books in the New Testament. Though the language is very simple and the vocabulary is small, making it one of the first books that students of Greek study in the original, the concepts are worthy of lifelong meditation. The young fisherman of Galilee whom Jesus called a "Son of Thunder" (Mark 3:17) is now the aged apostle of love and addresses Christians throughout the province of Asia, and ultimately the entire world. Tradition tells us that in his extreme old age when he could no longer minister the word, John was carried into the church and when asked for a word of wisdom, would invariably say, "Little children, love one another."

HOW 1st JOHN FITS TOGETHER

Letters as personal as 1st John will be variously divided by different scholars. Most outlines stress the theme of "fellowship" in some way or another and the following is a handy beginning for grasping the epistle:

(1) Conditions of Fellowship (1:1-2:2)
(2) Conduct of Fellowship (2:3-11)
(3) Enemies of Fellowship (2:12-27)
(4) Tests of Fellowship (2:28-3:24)
(5) Cautions of Fellowship (ch. 4)
(6) Results of Fellowship (ch. 5)

CONTEXT

John wrote the epistle to refute a form of the heresy of Gnosticism. This philosophy denied Christ's incarnation. It taught that Jesus was just a natural man, and the Divine Spirit came upon Him at His baptism, but left Him at the cross. This heresy also taught that all material substance was evil, and that only the spirit was good. They believed that man was lost because of being imprisoned in a material body. His only hope of salvation, they taught, was through self-knowledge.

John wrote the epistle as a restatement of the gospel. The message is that he who is born of God accepts the incarnation of Jesus Christ, the Son of God. He lives a life of righteousness, and this is evidenced by love for his brothers in Christ.

The apostle dwells on the spiritual and moral elements in Christianity rather than on external forms. He has very little to say about the church, church ordinances, church officers, or conduct of public worship. He emphasizes the union of believers with Christ. He thus dwells on faith, love, prayer, and eternal verities.

The epistle reveals the deep, abiding interest and intimacy the author has toward his children. Their interest is his interest; their joy is his joy; their struggle is his struggle.

John "the Elder" writing to his "little children" knew what the true gospel was. He was there when it began. He had seen, heard, and touched the incarnate Word of Life.

The Book of Jonah

Jonah is unique, being the only book among the prophets that consists chiefly of narrative (except for the second chapter, which is in the form of a psalm). Jonah's stay in the belly of the great fish is used by our Lord in the New Testament to picture His burial and resurrection. Although it has been traditional to speak of "Jonah and the whale," the Hebrew word here and the Greek word in the New Testament do not mean "whale".

There have been other historical incidents recorded of men (and even men on horseback!) swept overboard in the Mediterranean and swallowed whole by giant sharks. A few have lived to tell the story, as Jonah did, but this does not take away from the perfection of God's timing or from the other miracles in the book.

Unbelief has stumbled over the miraculous in this book, and some have even said that it is a parable, rather than history. There is nothing to indicate a parable, however, and Christ speaks of Jonah as a historical prophet who actually experienced the things recorded in this little book.

AUTHORSHIP

Jonah has traditionally been credited with being the author of this book named for him. Because of the personal information contained in the book, logic makes him the best candidate as author, although there is no absolute proof of his authorship.

CONTEXT

Jonah was active during the reign of Jeroboam ll. (793-753BC.). The northern kingdom fell in 722 BC. Based on these two historical facts and the logic that Jonah was the source of information, if not the author of the book, the consensus is that he would have written it prior to the fall of the northern kingdom and after the beginning of Jeroboam ll's reign. The best time frame for this book to have been written would be 790-722 BC.

HOW JONAH FITS INTO THE BIBLE

The book of Jonah illustrates God's love and concern for Gentiles even during the time of the favorable relationship the children of Israel had with God. It becomes a prelude to God's reaching out to the entire world through His Son Jesus Christ.

SUMMARY STATEMENT

God demonstrates His love for even His greatest enemies and for His angry and stubborn prophet.

KEY VERSE:

Ch. 2v9 "Salvation is of the Lord." God shows His love through His plan of salvation for Nineveh (and today through His plan of salvation in Christ Jesus).

HOW JONAH FITS TOGETHER

Initially we see Jonah rejecting God's call to reach a lost people (ch. 1). Even though Jonah attempts to run from God, he fails, resulting in his repentance (ch 2). Released from the belly of the fish, Jonah is re-commissioned to his great evangelistic calling, which results in the repentance of the people of Nineveh and the demonstration of God's grace (ch. 3). Finally, we see Jonah showing his anger and lack of compassion in sharp contrast to God's mercy and love while remaining just (ch. 4).

In Jonah we can see how bitter and unforgiving we can become when we are out of God's will. It is God's desire that none should perish.

Today is a good time for each of us to consider where we are in relationship to God's will for our lives. What a tragedy it would be if we were unforgiving, angry, and bitter persons.

The Second Book of Kings

AUTHORSHIP

To be sure 2nd Kings is adventuresome reading. But who wrote this fast-moving historical account of the two kingdoms? We do not know for certain who the human author is. There is no internal evidence; the author does not identify himself. The traditional view from the Jewish Talmud ascribes the book to the prophet Jeremiah. This seems most acceptable. Jeremiah is a logical candidate for several reasons:

(1) He was the last prophet of Israel's independence
(2) He would be moved to preserve the record of Israel's history.
(3) He demonstrated devotion to history in his own prophecy, the book that bears his name.
(4) There are similarities between 2nd Kings and the book of Jeremiah, not only in historical details but also in the style of writing as well. These reasons are not conclusive, but they do give us grounds for holding to Jeremiah as the author of 2nd Kings.

CONTEXT

1st and 2nd Kings recount four centuries of Israelite kings, from the death of David to the liberation of Jehoiachin from prison (971-560 BC) If you are looking for exciting reading-here it is! 2ND Kings reports to the world a most complete record of two tragedies in the national life of Israel:(1) the fall of Israel, the northern kingdom, in 722 BC; (2) the fall of the southern kingdom, Judah, and the burning of Jerusalem, in 586 BC.

HOW 2nd KINGS FITS INTO THE BIBLE

Actually, the history contained in 1st and 2nd Kings forms a single volume in the original Hebrew canon. The division into two books goes back to the Greek translation, called the Septuagint, and a Latin version called the Vulgate.

The Septuagint is designated by the Roman numerals, LXX, after the seventy translators who worked in the translation. All this goes back to between 285-247 BC. The Vulgate was a much later translation. A Christian scholar by the name of Jerome was commissioned by the bishop of Rome, in AD 383, to undertake a Latin translation of the Bible. In AD 392 Samuel and Kings were issued, and the entire Bible was complete in AD 405.

In both the Septuagint and the Vulgate, Samuel and Kings were divided quite arbitrarily, not even at any marked epoch in the historical narrative. It was more than likely for convenience of use and reference that the division was made.

On a more inspiring note, we see in 2 nd Kings the miracle ministry of the great prophet Elisha. His ministry was quite long, extending through the reigns of at least five kings of Israel (93-95 years). He was very useful to these kings as he was able to furnish insight and counsel that related to the affairs of Israel. His advice, however, was not always appreciated. He spoke to man from God and boldly confronted the evil, even of kings. But in all his miracle-working ministry, Elisha attested Jehovah to be the living God over Israel.

SUMMARY STATEMENT

The writer is saying to all generations that there are significant spiritual lessons to be learned from the way God acts and interacts in the lives and history of His people. The central theme to keep in mind is the fall of the kingdom.

HOW 2 nd KINGS FITS TOGETHER

What do we have in this book? It is simply a synchronized list of the kings of Israel and Judah, or is there a more fundamental purpose of its writing? The prophetic sayings throughout the book relate the events of that time to God and His governance over His people. The sins of the people are brought forth, their repentance is recorded, God's punishment is pronounced and His forgiveness is conveyed.

There are two major divisions in the book: (1) The Corruption of the Divided Kingdom (1-16); (2) The Retribution upon the Divided Kingdom (17-25).

The book of 2 nd Kings is truly the Word and Works of God. You will read not so much what He had to say, but what He did, in and through man-be he evil or good.

It seems that God does not deal immediate retribution to evil men today; but the teaching of 2nd Kings is still true; Man will reap what he sows.

The Gospel According to Mark

AUTHORSHIP

John Mark, nephew of Barnabas, was led by the Holy Spirit to write the book bearing his name, perhaps in Rome. Mark was a native of Jerusalem, where his mother Mary had a house in which the early Christians met. It was Mark's privilege to accompany his uncle Barnabas and the apostle Paul on the first missionary journey, but for some reason Mark did not complete the journey, causing a separation between Paul and Barnabas over Mark's defection. Fortunately, Mark later proved himself a worthwhile servant of the Lord, and it is widely believed that his Gospel embodies the reminiscences of the apostle Peter. In fact, the outline of the book seems similar to Peter's presentation in Acts.

HOW MARK FITS INTO THE BIBLE

Mark is thought by most modern scholars to be the oldest Gospel, although the traditional view is that Matthew, who wrote especially for the Jews, was first. Mark was definitely written before the destruction of Jerusalem (AD 70), and may have been written as early as the middle of the first century. Because of Mark's appeal to the Gentiles, his book forms a nice bridge between the Jewish-oriented Gospel of Matthew and the only books in the New Testament written by a Gentile, Luke and its companion volume, Acts.

KEY VERSE: 10:45

"For even the Son of Man did not come to be served, but to serve, and to give His life a ransom for many."

SUMMARY STATEMENT

Mark presents the Lord Jesus as the Servant of the Lord, and for this reason stresses action and deeds rather than words or family pedigree.

HOW MARK FITS TOGETHER

In light of the key verse, the Gospel of Mark may be divided into two parts, the first half stressing Christ's service (Chs. 1-10) and the second, His sacrificial death. (Chs. 11-16). Also, the book may be nicely divided according to the geography of Palestine: (1) Jesus' Preparation for the Ministry (1:1-13); (2) Jesus' Preaching in Galilee (1:14-9:50); (3) Jesus' Preaching in Perea (ch. 10); (4) Jesus' Passion and Resurrection at Jerusalem (Chs. 11-16).

CONTEXT

Because Gentile Romans were interested in power, action, and service, and not concerned with genealogy, as Jews would be, Mark omits the birth and childhood of Jesus. He immediately establishes Christ's deity by giving seventeen miracles showing His power over disease, nine miracles showing His power over nature, six miracles showing His power over demons, and three miracles proving His power over death. Christ is truly LORD over disease, demons, death and all nature.

Since the Roman mind was attuned to obedient, loyal servants, Mark uses the word euthus ("immediately") forty-two times, more than all the other New Testament writers combined. Christ indeed is our loyal Servant-Savior.

Let us study Mark and thank God that Christ, our Savior, loves us enough to minister to our every need.

The Book of Micah

The book of Micah was written by a country preacher who moved from the backwoods to the boulevards to preach to the cities. We know very little about him beyond the statement found in the first chapter: "The word of the Lord that came to Micah of Moresheth in the days of Jotham, Ahaz, and Hezekiah, kings of Judah" (1:1; see also Jer. 26:18; Mic. 1:14).

The name Micah means "Who is like Jehovah?", a name which is an index to his character. Micah had an exalted conception of the holiness, righteousness, and compassion of God. The heart of his book is expressed in the closing chapter: "Who is a God like You . . . ?" (7:18). (The unspoken answer, of course, is an exultant "None!") His writings indicate that he was a man of strong convictions, yet tenderhearted and compassionate. He spoke with courage to the sins of his day and called for a return of the people to the principles of God.

Micah is a thrilling book to read because it is filled with poetic beauty. It contains remarkable prophecy concerning Jerusalem and the future glory of that city. As proof that it is the Word of God, the book of Micah names the birthplace of the Savior; this passage prophesying the coming Messiah (5:2-5a), a brief poem of eight lines in Hebrew, is one of the most spiritual and exquisite passages in the Old Testament.

KEY VERSE: 6:8

"He has shown you, O man, what is good; and what does the Lord require of you but to do justly, to love mercy, and to walk humbly with your God?"

HOW MICAH FITS TOGETHER

Some have advocated that the book consists of three sermons, each beginning with the word Hear. According to this interpretation, the sermons deal with the coming judgment, the coming Deliverer, and the call to repentance today. By reading the book, however, one sees that there are not three but at least six uses of the word Hear (1:2; 3:1, 9; 6:1, 2, 9).

The book of Micah basically divides itself into two main parts. The first part, chapters 1-3, is a denunciation. God is against idolatry in high places as people worship things which they can manufacture such as clothes, houses, and money. He promises to destroy all these things. Covetousness is so rampant that people lie awake at night thinking on how they can get more things; then they awaken early in the morning to execute their greedy plans (2:1-2; cf. Amos 8:5-6).

The second main division, chapters 4-7, is consolatory. In the first part of chapter 4, there is a change of tone in Micah's preaching, as he seeks to console the people by turning from a message of judgment to a message of the future glories of Israel. Israel is to be gathered and delivered from Babylonian captivity. In chapter 5 Micah pleads for a return to spiritual worship and service. Sin and evil must be denounced and judged for people to receive the blessings of God. The last chapter of the book reveals Micah preaching and mourning for Israel's sins. Even the home has been invaded by deceit and hatred (7:5-6). The prophet then turns to God and confesses Israel's sins and counts on God's grace for the future (7:14-20). The only way for anyone-a nation or an individual-to receive the blessings of God is by repentance and confessions of sin.

The Book of Nahum

God will not tolerate perennial rebellion. Our God is truly long-suffering (2 Pet. 3:9); but in time His extended mercy is withdrawn and certain judgment comes like a whirlwind. No man can stand against the fierceness of God's wrath.

In the book of Nahum, God's forecast for punishment against Nineveh brings chills to our bones and revives our awesome reverence for our Holy God. Our God is shown here as a jealous God bent on divine justice. Never be mistaken: God is merciful but His wrath is sure and powerful.

AUTHORSHIP AND CONTEXT

The only reference in the Scriptures to "Nahum the Elkoshite" is in the first verse in this book. Elkosh was probably a village of Palestine, although some believe it may have been somewhere near Nineveh. Nahum prophesied sometime between the destruction of No Amon-ancient Thebes-in 663 BC (3:8-10) and Nineveh's fall in 612 BC.

Nineveh was the capital of the cruel Assyrian Empire, which almost a century before had carried the northern kingdom away into captivity (722 BC). Nahum may not have preached there, but only spoke about the city to the people of Judah (1:15)

His name in Hebrew means "Comfort" or "Consolation," and the ruin of this violent people would indeed be comforting to the often-victimized Judah. If he actually went, however, it would not be the first time God had spoken to Nineveh, for the prophet Jonah had been sent there one-and-a-half centuries before. But it would be the last time. Now it was in the purpose of God to visit judgment upon Nineveh, the capital of the empire that had been the rod of God's anger upon the northern kingdom of Israel.

HOW NAHUM FITS TOGETHER

Chapter 1 proclaims God's power and majesty as it is shown by His wrath against the evil city. Chapter 2 vividly describes the siege and destruction of Nineveh, in one of the most exciting passages of the Scriptures. Finally, Chapter 3 tells why Nineveh deserved God's judgment and how that judgment is inescapable.

KEY VERSES: 1:7, 8

"The LORD is good, a stronghold in the day of trouble; and He knows those who trust in Him. But with an overflowing flood He will make an utter end of its place, and darkness will pursue His enemies."

God's irrevocable indictments against Nineveh, that ruthless, bloodthirsty city, come like swift, hot arrows from the divine bow. Nineveh is an enemy of God. She has received evil counsel from the wicked. She is vile and despised, hated by all. She is a liar and a thief, full of false religion and the tyrannical abuse of power. Judgment against her is sure!

The prophet Jonah, fresh from the belly of a great fish, had preached repentance to Nineveh and she had indeed repented. But now, some 150 years later, the message of the prophet Nahum is not an offer to repent but a prophecy of impending judgment. God's wrath is pledged upon these sinners who had turned away from God. Their vileness, their hopeless pagan idolatry, their blatant self-reliance, their cocky ungodliness-all would be rewarded with destruction.

The book of Nahum provides a rare display of divine sarcasm. As the Neo-Babylonian Empire marches against Assyria, and a coalition of Medes and Chaldeans prepare to lay siege to the great city of Nineveh, God's prophet taunts the hated enemy: "Man the fort! Watch the road! Strengthen your flanks! Fortify your power mightily" (2:1). This challenge mocks a cruel tyrant who had long enslaved and oppressed the peoples of the ancient Near East. Now the destroyer will be destroyed! In the words of the Lord Jesus Christ: "All who take the sword will perish by the sword" (Matt. 26:52).

Nahum also gives us a forecast of the inevitable reaction of Nineveh to God's terrible judgment. It is a vivid portrait of a pitiful people who foolishly fought against our holy God. These sinners in the hands of an angry God are seen retreating in fear and agony. They run naked, leaving all their riches behind, fleeing like cowards, with no place to hide. Their pomp and pride and haughtiness are gone. Their kings and noblemen are dead, their people are scattered, and their enemies clap their hands, rejoicing. Nineveh is punished and her voice is silenced forever.

"It is a fearful thing to fall into the hands of the living God" (Heb. 10:31).

The Book of Obadiah

God's view of human pride and His response to it are just two of the important themes contained in Obadiah, the shortest prophesy in the Old Testament. The book is named after the prophet whose message it bears. The name Obadiah simply means "Servant of Jehovah."

Obadiah's prophecy is set against the background of the hatred which existed between Israel and Edom, a tension that had its origins in the marked differences between Jacob and Esau (Gen. 25:21-34).

The message of the book focuses on the nation of Edom, which had exploited its neighbors by extracting heavy taxes from the caravans forced to travel through its territory. It had engaged in slave trade (2 Chr. 28:17; Amos 1:6-9), and had acted treacherously toward Israel (Obadiah vv. 10-14). Edom's absolute control of the rugged territory southeast of the Dead Sea had produced a false sense of security and an arrogant disposition (v.3).

AUTHORSHIP

Although there are a number of individuals bearing the name Obadiah in the Old Testament, it is not possible to identify this prophet confidently with any of them. The straightforward and uncompromising nature of his prophecy, however, marks him as a man of courage.

CONTEXT

Obadiah did not identify any of the kings who reigned during his ministry. The date of this book, therefore, must be established by internal evidence alone. Obadiah's reference to the invasion of Jerusalem by "strangers" (v.11) has led some to associate this event with the great destruction of Judah and Jerusalem by the Babylonians in 586 BC. The prophet's description of

Jerusalem's humiliation is so unlike that of all the other prophets in scope and nature, however, that it seems better to relate the events of verses 10-14 with the raids on Jerusalem by the Philistines and Arabians during the reign of Jehoram of Judah (2 Chr. 21:16, 17). This would place the date of the book and the events described therein in the middle of the ninth century BC.

HOW OBADIAH FITS TOGETHER

The subject matter of Obadiah naturally divides into four parts, as follows: (1) The Certainty of Edom's Destruction (vv. 1-4); (2) The Character of Edom's Destruction (vv. 5-9); (3) The Cause of Edom's Destruction (v. 10-14); and (4) The Climax of Edom's Destruction: The Day of the Lord (vv. 15-21).

The dominant theme of the book is God's judgment upon Edom because of her sinful attitudes and actions. Pride was at the heart of Edom's sinful attitudes and God declared that He would humble the inhabitants of Edom before all the surrounding nations (vv. 1-9).

The Old Testament is filled with warnings against personal and national pride. The book of Proverbs, for example, gives special attention to the matter (Prov. 6:17; 11:2; 15:25; 16:5; 21:4, 24; 26:12; 29:23); the writer declares, "Pride goes before destruction, and a haughty spirit before a fall" (Prov. 16:18). The book of Obadiah illustrated exactly how God deals with the matter of pride in terms of historical realities.

While the condemnation of Edom dominates most of Obadiah's message, there is also a message of hope to the suffering Hebrews. The conclusion to the whole matter would be Israel's final triumph-the ultimate blessing of Zion and the people of God (vv. 17-21).

Even the most casual reading of Obadiah should produce a sense of awe for the perfection with which God accomplishes His purpose and upholds His moral standards. Nations which have rebelled against the rule of the Almighty have fallen in the past; those who choose to lift their voices in arrogant defiance against God will also fall in the future (Ps. 2).

The Book of Proverbs

The past three decades have seen a tragic emptiness and lack of direction in the Western world. Almost persistently, the old foundations have been eroded, and we are left with the dilemma that befell Israel during the time of the judges: "everyone did what was right in his own eyes" (Judges 17:6).

Alongside the aimlessness is a marvelous sign of hope. In the latter part of the twentieth century, a new worldwide sense of urgency for evangelism is setting the stage for the coming of the Lord Jesus. Accompanying this fervor for souls is an intense desire to know the Word of God.

One book that is being rediscovered in the Word of God is the book of Proverbs. It has often been neglected, yet in this library of God-given practical wisdom are the formulas for living a life of purpose and direction.

The supreme purpose of this book is to teach us that to know God personally is more important than everything else is (1:7). The goal of Proverbs, then, is to equip man for every good work (2 Tim. 3:15-17). Here godly, practical principles are set forth so that from them we may learn how to walk in righteousness, equity, and love.

KEY VERSE

The key to Proverbs hangs right inside the door in the first sentence (1:1-6), and the book's teaching is well stated in 1:7—"The fear of the Lord is the beginning of knowledge, but fools despise wisdom and instruction."

Proverbs is not a mere book of good manners. In its pages is the key to genuine living. To the youth, preparing to leave home, to the family member seeking to maintain godly order in the home, or to the leader concerned about social ills, the book gives one essential standard for making decisions: "Is this wisdom or folly? Does God lead in this path?"

The word proverb derives from the Latin words pro, meaning "for," and verb, meaning "word"; thus a proverb takes the place of a many-worded discourse. Proverbs are short, catchy truisms which are true because they come from God and are not to be discounted because of their brevity. They are to be weighed by their fullness, their superior value, and their applicability to the situations of life. To be conversant in other important books, but ignorant of the depth of this book, is infinite folly, for here is practical religion.

AUTHORSHIP

Solomon wrote the bulk of the Proverbs. This wisdom literature was begun by Solomon, passed around orally and in segmented writings, and probably finalized in its composition during Hezekiah's reign (25:1).

Proverbs in a general statement is the practical expression of our day-to-day living. Its purpose is to direct our daily, relational life just as the Psalms express our heart's worship of God. The Proverbs demonstrate how mankind is to live successfully, accomplish worthy goals by making right decisions, and please God in relationships with other people.

KEY WORD

The key word is wisdom. This wisdom derives from God as a gift (Chs. 2 and 8), but expresses itself in our dealings not only with God but with all others as well.

HOW PROVERBS FITS TOGETHER

There are three main divisions of the book, each beginning with a reminder that these are "the proverbs of Solomon." The divisions are: (1) A Father's Praise of Wisdom (Chs. 1-9); (2) A General Collection Concerning Prudence (10-24, written mostly by Solomon); and (3) A Collection from Hezekiah (25-31, written by Solomon, Agur, and others).

The ultimate desire of Proverbs is that we may be led to the One in whom "all the fullness" dwells (Col. 1:19), to claim Him as the source of all wisdom and knowledge, and to see the working out of "Christ in you, the hope of glory" (Col. 1:27). To that end may God bless you as you dig into this spiritual gold mine where God's wisdom is stored.

The Book of Ruth

The book of Ruth is the romance book of the Bible. It has all the dramatic love and action of a best-seller on the contemporary book list. The love affair in this story, however, is not the relationship of a young man and woman but rather the affection of a young woman, Ruth, and her mother-in-law, Naomi. Ruth and Naomi exemplify the love of kinship which is absent in the typical home of our present-day society. It gives a high ideal of wedlock and a sense of commitment to the family.

AUTHORSHIP

The writer of the book is unknown. It must have been written when the rule of the Judges had ended with the introduction of the monarchy. It came after the birth of David, and some conclude that Samuel wrote it. The book covers about ten years and stands as a kind of appendix to the book of Judges. The book of Ruth is the only one in the canon, which is completely devoted to the history of a woman.

SUMMARY STATEMENT

Ruth teaches the loyal love of God to the faithful minority, even in a time of spiritual decline.

THE PURPOSE OF RUTH

The purpose of this book is to trace the genealogy of David and ultimately of our Lord Jesus Christ. Ruth, who was a Gentile, married Boaz, a Jew. The story is a foreshadowing of the calling of the Gentiles to salvation. The Mosaic law shut off the Moabites, who therefore could be admitted only by God's grace. Ruth was related to Boaz by marriage; so are we related to Christ by the "marriage" of our human nature to His divine nature. As Boaz, who is a type of Christ, receives Ruth with love and tenderness, so our Lord receives us to Himself in forgiveness and cleansing so that we may find rest in Him.

KEY WORD AND KEY VERSE

Although the word rest is found only twice in the book of Ruth (1:9, 3:18), yet the thought permeates the entire story. In the East, the position of the unmarried woman is dangerous; only in the house of a husband can she be sure of respect and protection. Elimelech forsook rest when he left the Promised Land. To leave Moan for Bethlehem seemed an impossible path to rest, as Naomi gravely and tactfully hinted, but God's ways are not man's ways. Ruth found rest through redemption and union with Christ our Divine Redeemer. The key verse of Ruth is 2:12—"The Lord repay your work, and a full reward be given you by the Lord God of Israel, under whose wings you have come for refuge."

The lessons to be learned from the book of Ruth are pronounced. Israel was out of the will of God and thus suffered the punishment of God. God dealt with a Gentile who married a Jew (Boaz) and completed the lineage of Christ, thus showing the universality of God's redemption of men to form His family. Boaz is a picture of Christ who is the Lord of the harvest and who provides spiritual rest and refreshment for all who come to His feet in submission. Naomi had backslid and found the only way to peace was back in the will of God with His people. Thus it is with all of us: the world cannot satisfy the deepest needs of our lives; only in Christ are they met.

Perhaps the best-known passage in Ruth is found in 1:16-17: "Entreat me not to leave you, or to turn back from following after you; for wherever you go, I will go; and wherever you lodge, I will lodge; your people shall be my people, and your God, my God. Where you die, I will die, and there will I be buried. The Lord so do to me, and more also, if anything but death parts you and me."

The Songs of Solomon

AUTHORSHIP

Solomon wrote 1,005 songs, according to 1 Kings 4:32, but the Song of Solomon is the only one that has survived. We know it is the finest because the expression "Song of Songs" (the book's Hebrew title, taken from 1:1 is the Hebrew way of making a superlative. It means, therefore, "the most exquisite, or best song." It is, in fact, one of the loveliest poems in all literature, if not the loveliest. Tradition says that Solomon wrote the Song when he was young, in his first experience of true love, before the multiple political marriages and the concubinage that later so damaged his spiritual life and testimony (1 Kin. 11:8-10).

CONTEXT

The book dates from about 965 BC, and tells the true story of King Solomon's love for a lovely country maiden, a Shulamite. An alternate theory posits a love triangle-Solomon the king trying to steal the maiden from her beloved rustic shepherd. Such a situation is most unlikely, however, since it would make the king of Israel the villain of a book named after himself.

HOW THE SONG OF SOLOMON FITS INTO THE BIBLE

Love is the greatest of personal qualities (1 Cor. 13:13), and surely the mutual love of a man and wife is one of the most important of God-ordained loves. Today there is a popular theory that the Song of Solomon is a "marriage manual" for young couples. Aside from the fact that the poem is too subtle to be a "manual" for anything not already understood, neither the Jewish temple nor the Christian church has ever regarded the book in this light. The Jews, in fact, forbade the reading of the Song until a man was thirty years of age! Ancient Jews saw the book as a portrayal of Israel's relationship to the Lord as the wife of Jehovah (cf. Is. 54:5; Jer. 2:2; Ezek. 16:8-14; Hos. 2:16-20).

The Christian church extended this view to refer specifically to the Lord Jesus, the person of the Godhead who, for the love of God, came to earth to seek and to save the lost. Luke 24:27 says that Christ expounded to the Emmaus travelers "in all the Scriptures the things concerning Himself" (emphasis added). Since the chapter and verse divisions are man-made and late, there is no need to say that Christ is specifically predicted or typified in each individual verse of the Holy Writ, but it certainly is inconceivable that an entire book of the Bible could have nothing of Christ in it. Luther, as is well known, saw Christ as the key to all Bible books, and in this he was no doubt correct. Also, 2 Corinthians 11:2, Ephesians 5:24, and Revelation 19:7-9 and 21:9 all picture the Church as a bride and Christ as the husband, which fits in with the general flow of the Song of Solomon.

SUMMARY STATEMENT

The Song of Songs poetically relates the growing love, the separation, and the final consummation of love between King Solomon and the Shulamite maiden, giving literally poetic praise of married love and spiritually a picture of the love of God for Israel and of Christ for His Bride, the Church.

KEY WORDS AND KEY VERSE

The key words in the Song of Songs are love and beloved. Several verses would make good theme verses, such as 2:4 and 7:10, but perhaps the best verse to express the theme of the book is 8:7—"Many waters cannot quench love, nor can the floods drown it. If a man would give for love all the wealth of his house, it would be utterly despised."

HOW THE SONG OF SOLOMON FITS TOGETHER

As a poem, the Song is difficult to outline, and no two interpreters agree on the exact flow of action. It is a unified poem, however, as is shown by unity of character and by the repetition of such refrains as "I charge you, O daughters of Jerusalem . . ." The book may be broadly divided as follows:

Love Beginning (1:1-3:5); Love Uniting (3:6-5:1); Love Struggling (5:2-7:10); Love Progressing (7:11-8:14).

Among the varied books in the Word of God, the Song of Songs is unique. This unified dramatic poem is full of observations and comparisons involving plants and animals. In its eight short chapters, Solomon mentions fifteen animals, twenty-one plants, and fifteen geographical sites from Lebanon in the north to Egypt in the south.

The Song has been an inspiration to centuries of poets and musicians. Hymns such as "Emmanuel's Land" and many others draw heavily on its wording. The titles "Rose of Sharon" and "Lily of the Valley" are often applied by poets to the Lord Jesus, but in context they are feminine comparisons by the Shulamite maiden of herself with common field flowers (2:1). The titles from this book that are most suitable for our Lord are "Altogether Lovely" (5:16) and "Chief Among Ten Thousand" (5:10).

The First Epistle of Paul
The Apostle to The Thessalonians

AUTHORSHIP

1st Thessalonians is considered one of Paul's earliest letters, written about AD 51. It reveals the apostle as a tender, affectionate man with a great concern for the spiritual welfare of his converts. This letter also shows the purity of Paul's motive, his compassion, and dedication. His innermost feelings are manifest in these pages.

CONTEXT

1st Thessalonians interestingly shows the rich doctrine found even in the primitive evangelism of the early church. Apparently the apostle Paul had spent only one month teaching the Thessalonians basic Christian truths when he was in their city (Acts 17:2). In that time, the people were enlightened from total heathenism to the Christian hope. A strong point in Paul's teaching throughout this epistle was to give them hope while living in anticipation of the Lord's return. He repeatedly challenges them to a practical Christian walk in preparation for this great event. The passage, 4:13-5:11, is one of the fullest New Testament developments of this crucial truth.

As Paul reflects on his personal experiences with this church, he points out several areas of weakness-laziness and sexual sins in particular. Paul also encourages the believer to live in faith, love, and hope as he anticipates the imminent return of our Lord and Savior Jesus Christ.

HOW 1 THESSALONIANS FITS INTO THE BIBLE

1st Thessalonians has a unique contribution to the New Testament as a bridge between Paul's missionary work in Acts and the predictions of the future in Revelation. No other book tells us as much about the rapture of the church as 1 Thessalonians (4:13-18). It also has a great deal to say about the day of the Lord (5:1-11). The coming of Christ is so important in this book that every single chapter has something to say about it.

HOW 1 THESSALONIANS FITS TOGETHER

The two outstanding major sections of 1 Thessalonians are (1) Personal Experience (Chs. 1-3) and (2) Practical Exhortation (Chs. 4, 5).

Many models are pictured in this great book. Chapter 1 gives us a view of the model church and virtues of the Christian life. Chapter 2 gives a distinctive coverage of the model servant and his reward. The character traits of a model believer are clearly portrayed in chapter 3 in the feelings expressed toward the brethren within the church at Thessalonica. In chapters 4 and 5 we have an example of the model walk of sanctification and the ultimate hope of the believer while eagerly awaiting the Lord's return.

The final analysis of this book is the reflection of Christ as seen in the believer's hope of salvation both now and at His coming. When Christ returns, He will deliver (1:10; 5:4-11) reward (2:19), perfect (3:13), resurrect (4:13-18), and sanctify (5:23) all who trust Him. What a tremendous reward the believer has!

The Third Epistle of John

3rd John is a unique gold mine. Though marked by its brevity, this book deals with the biggest of problems and power struggles in the church. The secret of the greatest joy is found in its words. John's third epistle tells us plainly whom Christians should support. The book deals with a quest of all men-assurance of salvation. The teacher finds in 3 rdJohn a helpful message on "Three Typical Church Members": Gaius, the beloved believer; Diotrephes, the domineering disciple; and Demetrius, the complimented Christian.

AUTHORSHIP

Like 1st and 2nd John, John's third epistle was penned by the apostle of love when he was an old man, probably between AD 85-95.

HOW 3 rd JOHN FITS INTO THE BIBLE

Though very short, this epistle would be missed if it were not there. It gives a colorful glimpse into the life and problems of the late first century church. Its warning against church dictators is much needed today in some circles.

HOW 3 rd JOHN FITS TOGETHER

The outline of the book follows the three main characters:

(1) Greeting to the Godly and Generous Gaius (vv. 1-8)
(2) Denunciation of the Dictatorial Diotrephes (vv. 9-11)
(3) Commendation of Demetrius and Complementary Close (vv. 12-14)

KEY WORD

As with 2 nd \John, the key world in 3 rd John is truth. It appears six times in the book's 296 words. The word true is also found once, giving seven mentions of truth in this single chapter. 3 John underscores Martin Luther's resolve, "Peace if possible, but truth at any rate." Truth is the foundation of love in a Christian fellowship: "Gaius, whom I love in truth" (v.1). Truth, in our heart, liberates us from the enslaving passions of life: "the truth that is in you, just as you walk in the truth" (v.3). Verse 4 says, "I have no greater joy than to hear that my children walk in truth"; the greatest joy a Christian worker can ever experience is winning another person and leading them to "walk in truth."

A power struggle within the church resulted from Diotrephes' violation of the truth. He sought "to have the preeminence" (v.9). The high-handed methods of some men in modern church life were present in this early church. Diotrephes, like Lucifer, asserted his authority above the authority of the truth. He expelled members from the church on the basis of whom they associated with.

By contrast, Demetrius is held up as an ideal disciple, having a good testimony from men and "from the truth itself" (v.12). Such a man, who obeys the truth, has assurance he is of God. The man who disobeys the truth proves he has not seen God (v.11). Horace Mann said, "Keep one thing forever in view—the truth; and if you do this, though it may seem to lead you away from the opinion of men, it will assuredly conduct you to the throne of God."

Pilate once considered John's "truth," asking, "What is truth?" But his mind wandered to other matters, and he arose and left before he found the answer. Emerson said, "God offers to every mind its choice between truth and repose. Take which you please-you can never have both."

Dig deep in the truth of 3 rd Epistle of John. The hard work will bring a rich reward.

The Second Epistle of Paul
The Apostle to Timothy

AUTHORSHIP

All the evidence says that the apostle Paul wrote 2 nd Timothy. So says the letter, so said the early church. Not until modern times has there been a dissenting voice, and Paul's authorship has never had any justifiable criticism. The evidence of the Epistles themselves shows Paul as the writer.

Paul's writings reveal the characteristics of a man of strong emotion. He would be very stern (Gal 3:1-5; Acts 23:2, 3). But with profound tenderness he writes to Timothy, his "beloved son" (1:2; cf. Gal 4:19, 20). As a warm and personal letter, it has much in common with 1 Timothy, Titus, and Philemon.

The most probable date is the spring of AD 68. Nero killed himself in early June of that year and Paul was surely put to death before that date.

In this letter Paul instructs Timothy how to carry on the work of God after the apostle's death. The emphasis is on the great apostasy and social corruptions which will exist in the latter days of the church. In this, Paul's last epistle, there is a mellow wisdom and a sereneness of purpose in the profound triumph of Paul's spirit over all opposition. Confident in the blessed hope of the Lord's return and his own reward (4:8), he exhorts and instructs the young pastor to be a good soldier, as faithful as Christ was and as Paul has been.

HOW 2 nd TIMOTHY FITS INTO THE BIBLE

2 nd Timothy is Paul's farewell letter, not only to Timothy, but to all the apostle's millions, and by now literally billions, of readers through the centuries. It is his last letter as he faces the Roman sword, but he is ready. He has finished his race and kept the faith.

KEY VERSE:

2:3—"You therefore must endure hardship as a good soldier of Jesus Christ."

HOW 2ND TIMOTHY FITS TOGETHER

An outline based on the "good soldier" theme is:

(1) Greeting and Thanks for Timothy (1:1-7)
(2) The Good Soldier's Enlistment (1:8-18)
(3) The Good Soldier's Qualities (2:1-26)
(4) The Good Soldier's Apostate Enemies (ch. 3)
(5) The Good Soldier's Charge (4:1-5)
(6) The Good Soldier's Rewards (4:6-18)
(7) Final Greetings (4:19-22)

CONTEXT

In this letter, Paul reveals something of his circumstances at the time of writing. As a religious outlaw, Paul had been brought to the Mamertine Prison at Tome. Arrested on a double charge, he was not this time the victim of Jewish hate or Judaizing jealousy, but rather of Gentile intervention in what Nero considered an assault on the worship of the old gods in general and emperor worship in particular. Moreover, blaming the Christians for the great conflagration that took place in Rome in AD 64, it was not difficult to accuse Paul of complicity in the burning of the city and so get him to Rome.

Charged with these capital crimes, Paul was not now allowed the liberty of his own hired house, as he was at his first arrest in Acts 28. Confined in the dungeon, he was cold and lonely. He desired the cloak that he left with Carpus at Troas (4:13), and dreaded the prospect of another winter without it (4:21). He had already had his first court appearance and had escaped the mouths of the lions (4:16). Few of his friends dared to visit Paul, for now it was a crime to be a Christian, but Onesiphorus sought until he found him (1:16-18). Demas had forsaken him (4:10), and only Luke was with him.

We do not have a written account of Paul's death, but he was expecting to be led out soon to execution (4:6). Tradition tells us he was executed on the Ostian Road outside the city of Rome; so says Caius, quoted in Eusebius, Ecclesiastical History, 2:25. As a Roman citizen, he would be beheaded. Was Luke there? Let us hope so! When all others failed, Jesus was with him (4:17). Christ had not failed Paul in all the years since He stopped him on the Damascus Road, saved him and "revealed" to him the gospel of the Son of God (Gal. 1:11, 12).

The Epistle of Paul The Apostle to Titus

AUTHORSHIP

The first verse of the letter identifies Paul as the author and is confirmed by the contents as well as by church tradition from earliest days. Only in modern times have men attacked the Pauline authorship, and then largely through unbelief.

CONTEXT

The epistle appears to have been written from either Macedonia or Philippi during the period between Paul's first and second imprisonments, which would date it at approximately AD 63 or 64. According to 3:12 Paul was preparing to spend the winter in Nicopolis, on the west coast of Greece.

HOW TITUS FITS INTO THE BIBLE

Titus, along with 1st and 2 nd Timothy, makes up what we know as the Pastoral Epistles. The goals of Paul in writing this particular epistle included correcting false doctrine, motivating the recipients toward good works, and establishing order in the churches. He encourages Titus to do this by means of good, sound teaching (2:1).

SUMMARY STATEMENT

Titus is to speak the things, which are proper for sound doctrine: correct false doctrines, do good works, and establish order in the churches.

HOW TITUS FITS TOGETHER

Sound doctrine, good works, and church order are the goals of Paul in this epistle and it may be divided to reflect them in this manner: (1) the first four verses establish Paul's authority; (2) the rest of chapter 1 consists of instruction for the appointment and selection of church leaders; (3) chapter 2 contains Paul's exhortation and instructions for sound doctrine among the saints; and (4) chapter 3 provides the conclusion to the epistle.

The epistle to Titus was written for the purpose of instructing him in how to deal with the issues that concerned Paul at that time. The fact that Titus had been successful as an emissary of Paul in the past is reflected by his accomplishments at the church in Corinth. All records reveal him to be a man used by God to help overcome problems that had risen at a critical point in the growth of the early church.

The Book of Zephaniah

AUTHORSHIP AND CONTEXT

Zephaniah's name means "Jehovah Hides," i.e., shelters or protects. This great-great-grandson of the good King Hezekiah prophesied during the reign of King Josiah of Judah (640-608 BC), including Josiah's reformation which began in 621 B C. He was also related to King Josiah, who was a great-grandson of Hezekiah. Zephaniah thereby probably had access to the king's court and would have been influential in helping to bring about the great reformation, which unfortunately was more superficial than real. He was also a contemporary of Jeremiah, Nahum, and Habakkuk.

KEY VERSE:

"Seek the LORD, all you meek of the earth, who have upheld His justice. Seek righteousness, seek humility. It may be that you will be hidden in the day of the Lord's anger."

HOW ZEPHANIAH FITS TOGETHER

Rampant lawlessness, profaned worship, deceitful prophets, and virtually extinct religious convictions among the people occasioned this prophet's message. Its theme is "the day of the Lord," a phrase repeated many times. Zephaniah was a flaming evangelist who preached effectively a message burning with rebuke to a people reluctant to respond. In the midst of severe denunciation, he called for repentance which alone could save the nation from impending doom. Finally, his thunder and sternness gave way to sweetness and love, joy, and triumph, rest and salvation, as he foretold the bright future that would ultimately be Judah's.

This book may thus be divided according to its chapter breaks: chapter 1 proclaims God's coming retribution for the people's sins, chapter 2 seeks their repentance, and chapter 3 predicts their ultimate restoration. Terror turns to tenderness with a promise of redemption in the last twelve verses, and thus this prophet of doom reveals the heart of God, the goodness of the Lord, and the tenderness of His love. Affliction gives way to salvation and praise.

Bread and Brotherhood

TEXT: *If I have eaten my morsel alone.* JOB 31:17

The author of the Book of Job attempted to deal with the problem of evil. Until then the usual way of explaining suffering and evil was that they befell a man who had sinned, that they were the just consequences of wrong behavior. Job's comforters—who turned out not to be very comforting—tried to get Job to admit that he had sinned. This would have explained the loss of all his property, the death of his family, and the disease that afflicted him. Job stubbornly denied sinning. In the thirty-first chapter he answers his so-called comforters by saying that if he had done the things of which he was accused, then he could be justly punished.

Strangely enough, one of the sins that he lists is that of eating alone.

For us in the western world today, where eating has neither the ceremony nor significance it had in Job's day, we are puzzled when Job seemed so concerned about eating alone. The dining table for us is another filling station. Eating is a matter of stuffing our stomachs, and we do it as dispassionately as a man has his gas tank refilled.

But to the Oriental mind in the day of Job, *bread was sacramental*, not in the sense of any religious dogma, but in the sense that bread was more than just bread.

In the first place, bread was sacramental because man did not get it by himself. It was grown. Growing grain was a cooperative venture between man and God, the Lord of creation. In our day, especially those of us who live in town or cities, we are likely to think that machines make everything, including food. But it isn't. It never was.

> Back of the loaf is the snowy flour,
> And back of the flour the mill,
> And back of the mill is the wheat and the shower
> And the sun and the Father's will.

Bread is sacramental, too, because it is a social product. If Job had been a peasant, which he was not, he still would have been dependent on others. What was it that protected his fields, his vineyards, and his herds from marauders, from the pillaging of thieves? The community. Who was it that planted and harvested the grain? Who was it that prepared and served his bread? Others, on whom he was as dependent as we are. Food is a social product even more in our own day. When you buy a bag of flour or a loaf of bread, ten thousand hands and more have had something to do with it, from a grain of wheat to the flour or bread.

This reminds me of an incident that happened to a missionary to Africa shortly after his arrival on the field. He was on an expedition through the continent with an old native who had been associated with the mission for some years. They stopped for rest at noon, after a long morning on the trail. Mr. McDowell, full of American vim and vigor, ate his lunch in a hurry and began chafing over his companion's delay. Meanwhile, the old African continued blandly eating his meal with full deliberation. "Have patience," he pleaded. "Do not ask me to hurry. Don't you see I am eating my wife?"

To the young man fresh on the field that remark had an ominous sound. He looked apprehensively at the old man, wondering if perhaps his religion was only skin deep, after all. An explanation was soon forthcoming. "My wife fixed this lunch for me. She spent her time and her strength upon it. Part of her love and her life went into it. Do you want me to gulp it down with no thought or respect for her?"

You remember David at the cave of Abdullam. Word came to him that the enemy had taken possession of Bethlehem. Bethlehem! There swept over him a surge of homesickness at the very word. He could close his eyes and see the city of his youth. He could hear voices long since forgotten. He could see the crowd gathered at sunset about the curb of the well by the city gate. Hardly knowing that he spoke aloud, he sighed: "Oh that I might have a drink of the water of the well that is by that gate of Bethlehem!"

Next day three of his devoted followers brought to him a cup filled with the water. It was, they explained, water from the well of which he had spoken. Over the hills they had gone the night before, weary and dangerous miles. Through the lines of the enemy they had crept, where capture would have meant instant death; and then back. Three lives risked gladly, and without a murmur, for the joy of satisfying the whim of a leader they loved.

When the truth dawned on him, he was almost speechless with humility. Tears must have filled his eyes as he looked down into the cup. He shook his head. "I cannot drink it!" he exclaimed. "It is the blood of three men. It is too sacred just to drink." And he poured it out on the sand as an offering of gratitude to Almighty God.

Every day you and I eat the bodies and drink the blood of men and women who have spent their strength that we might have the means of life. The words of Our Lord come to my mind: "This is my body broken for you." In this sense bread is a sacrament.

Job also felt guilty if he had eaten alone because he recognized that brotherhood is not just an idea. Brotherhood is an experience that is real, and *it has an economic basis*. Food is a symbol of all the material things that a man needs to live, including clothing and shelter. That's why Job said in the verses immediately following the text: "If I have seen any perish for want of clothing, or any poor without covering; if his loins have not blessed me, and if he were not warmed with the fleece of my sheep . . . then let mine arm fall from my shoulder blade, and mine arm be broken from the bone." It was incongruous to Job that he should enjoy the blessings of life while others were destitute.

Food is the basic requirement in living. It is not surprising to read that out in Texas where men have used up the reservoir of water underground for crop irrigation, a barrel of water brings more than a barrel of oil. Before man needs oil he needs water and food. The first request for material things in the Lord's prayer is for bread: "Give us this day our daily bread." "Whenever we pray, 'give us this day our daily bread,'" says Dr. E. M. Poteat, "we give assent to one of the major premises on which social life must rest . . . Sharing the physical goods of the earth is as mandatory upon the Christian as preaching the gospel. It is, indeed, properly understood as a part of it."

Jesus so identified himself with the needs of men that he could say: "Inasmuch as you did it unto one of the least of these, you did it unto me." In fact, as presented in the closing chapters of Matthew, this was the test of whether men were his disciples.

There are those today who hastily condemn the Russian experiment in communal living. It hasn't succeeded, and it is wrong. But it is not wrong because it says that there must be an economic basis for life, that all men must have the necessities of living. It is wrong because they think that man can live by bread alone. However, they are no more in error than those who think that you can have brotherhood without any attention or concern about the elemental needs of man. The Kingdom of God is more than a concept. It is not just a Sunday fellowship. Brotherhood is that which men are able to create and achieve in daily intercourse with one another. If it is true that man does not live by bread alone, it is equally true that he must have bread.

One other thing troubled Job about eating alone, that is, *that eating together is the highest expression of fellowship*. So much was this true in Job's day that the host was obligated to protect the guest for twenty-four hours after he had eaten a meal. Eating together today is the highest expression of fellowship. Whenever we wish to honor our friends we invite them to a meal.

Yet just as it is the finest gesture of friendship, it is likewise the surest social stigma to eat with the wrong people. Every generation of people everywhere has its social outcasts.

They had them in Jesus' day, and one of the social sins that he committed was to eat with them. Poor Jesus! He was blacklisted as readily as you or I would be if we ate with the wrong people. Thus they said of Jesus: "He eats with publicans and sinners." He not only disgraced himself, but he in turn became an outcast.

The test of brotherhood is eating together. Thus on the last night of Jesus' earthly life when he had finished the meal of the annual Passover Feast, whether by forethought or the inspiration of the moment, he took some of the unleavened bread and the wine and gave it to the disciples saying: "as oft as you eat the bread and drink the cup, do it in remembrance of me." It is not accidental that one of the first occasions when Jesus was recognized after the resurrection was when two men invited a stranger to supper only to discover "in the breaking of bread" that the stranger was the risen Christ.

The early followers of Jesus understood it to mean that when they ate together they were to remember him, and they did. For a long while the Lord's supper was a regular meal, as Paul tells us in his letter to the Corinthians. Not until churches outgrew the households in which they first met, and the size of the group made it impractical, did they substitute the symbolic for the actual meal.

One of the ironic commentaries on the history of the Christian Church is that the observance which Jesus instituted to keep men together should become such a source of division among us, so that today there are four or five of the largest bodies of Christians who refuse to eat together at the Lord's table, and who, in the name of Christ, exclude all others. This is neither the time nor the place to discuss the doctrinal differences that account for this division among us. My point, however, is that Jesus said that the one place above all places men should remember him was in the breaking of bread. For it is here, as we all know, in the matter of eating bread, that men are either united or divided with all the miserable consequences that result from such division.

Jesus came into the world to create in men a sense of community, and to redeem them from all the evil that prevents their realizing it. Salvation is not just a vertical relationship, an affair between man and God. It is this. It is also a horizontal relationship, an affair between man and the other men about him. The Kingdom of God is not a man making his pilgrimage to the Holy City alone. It is a social concept. The church is not a boarding house nor a bus stop where men are accidentally brought together without obligation to the other. The church is a community of men and women who know themselves bound to God and to each other, like-minded and mutually dedicated.

Whenever we pray the Lord's Prayer, we are likely to think that Jesus gave this to his disciples as a public prayer. On the contrary, Jesus told them to pray the prayer in private. This makes it all the more significant. Nowhere in the prayer is the personal pronoun used in the singular, but always in the plural: "Our Father . . . our daily bread . . . our debts." When we pray the Lord's prayer we stretch out our hands to others about us as we make, not our individual, but our common supplication. To drop hands is to break faith. Nothing would seem more pitiful than someone praying: "Give *me* this day *my* daily bread," as if others about him had not the same need for bread.

In olden times a Scottish village in the highlands always kept a sentinel on watch lest an enemy take the people by surprise. High up on the mountainside he kept watch. If ever he saw the enemy, he would come to the hillside overlooking the village, and cupping his hands to his mouth, cry: "Shoulders together!" At this signal all the men would come together and stand as one man against a common enemy. Would God that in our day we could discover the sense of community that makes men brothers, that we could feel the incongruity and sinfulness of eating alone, as Job did. Then, and only then, may we expect him to be known of us in the "breaking of bread."

Calvary's Armistice

TEXT: *Having made peace through the blood of His cross.* Col. 1:20

PEACE! What a beautiful word it is; and when it comes after war, peace is a beautiful fact.

The signing of the Armistice in the Wood of Compiegne by the Allied and German plenipotentiaries brought to a close the most fearful war that the world had ever seen up to that time. It was a war in which the earth reeled, the sun was turned into darkness, and the moon into blood. Millions had fallen in battle, or died of wounds; millions had been left maimed and wounded; millions destitute and homeless, and millions were left brokenhearted. No wonder the earth rejoiced when the tidings were flashed around the globe that the cruel war had come to an end. Out of the blood and tears of humanity appeared the beautiful iridescent rainbow of peace.

The commemoration of the signing of the Armistice and the conclusion of the First World War brings to our mind another war, the war of sin against God and against man, and the armistice which was signed on Calvary.

The Peace of Versailles was signed in the famous palace of Louis XIV, which stands in the midst of rich gardens, with fountains flinging their silvery waters towards the sky. In the Gallerie des Glaces, with the representatives of all the great nations of the world assembled, the Treaty of Peace was signed. It was in the same hall that William I was crowned Emperor of Germany at the close of the War of 1870.

But the Treaty of Peace between God and man was signed on the Cross; signed not in ink, but in Immanuel's blood, while the heavens wondered and the earth shook and the sun veiled his face. The Treaty of Peace signed at Versailles affected all the nations which were at war with Germany; but the treaty of Peace signed at Calvary took in all ages, all races, all worlds, for, as St. Paul puts it, "It pleased the Father that in Him should all fullness dwell, and having made peace through the blood of His Cross, by Him to reconcile all things unto himself; by Him, I say, whether they be things in earth or things in heaven."

This war between man and God is as ancient as the fall of man, and as universal as the human race. When nations prepare for war, it occasions great excitement and rumor throughout the world. Newspapers display the tidings in flaring headlines. But the greatest and oldest and most widespread, most deadly, and most devastating of all wars, the war of sin, or man's war against God, receives hardly the slightest notice. This is because the whole human race is involved in this war, and has been involved in it throughout the history of the world.

Sin is the shadow cast by man wherever we find the human race. There is a reluctance on the part of men to face the deep facts of life, and one of the darkest and the deepest is this fact of sin. Sin is the breaking of the divine law, and therefore, the source of all human misery. What fact can be deeper and darker than this? What is it that casts so heavy a shadow across the path of man? What is it that poisons his cup, clouds the sky of his life, burdens his back, and fills his heart with sorrow? It is the fact of sin. The greatest of all delusions, the saddest of all self-deceptions, is that we have no sin. The faded sense of sin, and with it the feeling men have that they do not need a Saviour, that the Armistice signed on Calvary has no application for them, is only an evidence of the moral injury and decay which has overtaken man. Sin, or moral sin, is the fountain and source of the woes and sufferings of mankind. At war with God, man is at war with his fellowman, and at war with himself. "He that sinneth against God wrongeth his own soul." The earth has been devastated in the past, is being devastated today, and will be devastated in the ages to come by cruel and bloody wars. But there has never been a war, and there never will be a war which was not caused by this other war which underlies all wars and is the source of them, the war of man against God. Therefore, since men are engaged in this war against God, the world's great need is not education, or political organizations, or social amelioration, but reconciliation, peace with God.

In the midst of this war which takes in all nations and all ages, there come the tidings of peace to all men; an armistice has been signed on Calvary. Had peace not been offered, this war would have destroyed mankind.

Earth has no spot so sacred as the place where the divine armistice was signed by Christ in behalf of God. Thousands have gone to the quiet spot in the midst of the dense forest at Compiegne where the representatives of Germany and the Allied Armies met and signed the Armistice. There is nothing there, save the inscriptions, to remind one of the cruel and devastating war which there came to an end. All that one saw was the beauty of the forest, and all that one heard was the song of the birds in the tops of the trees, as they moved in the summer wind. But the thoughts of mankind will ever halt at Calvary.

There is a green hill far away,
Without the city wall,
Where our dead Lord was crucified
Who died to save us all.

Here the representative of God and of man was the same Divine Person, the God-man, even Jesus Christ. In the Armistice of November 11th, 1918, Marshal Foch signed for the Allied Government and the delegated German representatives for Germany. But in the peace signed in Calvary, Christ represented both God and man. God was in Christ, reconciling the world unto Himself.

"Couldn't anyone else have died for me just as well?" asked one to whom I was trying to explain the peace of Calvary. No; none other could have done what Christ did. In the first place, Christ died for man as a sinner. For a friend, for a good man, to save one from danger and peril, a man might lay down his life, but the marvel of Christ's death on the Cross was that He died for sinners. God commendeth His love toward us, in that while we were yet sinners Christ died for us.

The second reason why no one else could have died for us, and established peace between man and God, is that no one else could be what Christ was, and is, God in Christ. Therefore, what He did on the Cross has infinite value. He took on Himself as the representative of man all the responsibility of the war against God, and therefore all the guilt of the sinner; and as the representative of God, as the Son of God, and therefore truly God, Christ had the authority to make peace between God and Man. There is no Gospel, no message of redemption or of hope, in the mere fact that a good and noble man was tortured and crucified on the cross. But there is a Gospel, there is redemption, and there is hope in the fact that God was in Christ, and that Christ on the Cross bore in His own body the penalty upon sin, that is, the penalty which every sinner bears.

The problem of God was how to deal with sin, how to uphold the moral order of the world, to declare His righteousness and yet at the same time pardon the sinner. And not only pardon him, but make those who were the enemies of God His friends. In this great undertaking God did not deal lightly with sin. There was no ignoring of the fact of war and sin.

The world rejoiced when the Treaty of Versailles was signed. It seemed as if a new foundation had been built for the peace and welfare of the world. Now we know better. The Peace of Versailles could not put an end to war among the nations.

But the peace of Calvary goes deeper. When Absalom had murdered his brother, and was living in exile, it was not hard for Joab to persuade the mourning king and father, David, to be reconciled to Absalom and call him home again. But it was only a surface reconciliation. The heart of Absalom was not dealt with at all, and in a short time he conspired against his father and drove him from this throne. But the peace of God, signed on Calvary, went far deeper than that. It deals with the heart of man, the sinner and the exile, and makes him, once an enemy, and separated from God, now the friend of God.

It was to do this great work of making peace, of reconciling man to God, that Christ came into the World. God was in Christ reconciling man to himself. The heathen religions all were based upon the idea of attempting to reconcile God to man. Hence, all their altars, and all their dark and bloody rites. But the Gospel of Christ declares that God is reconciled to man, and now offers man the opportunity to be reconciled to God. God's enemies are to be made His friends.

That was the last thing Christ did in this world before He died. A thief and a robber who hung at His side on that awful day, and who at first had reviled Him and mocked Him, now prayed to Him, and asked Him to give them a place in His Kingdom. "Lord Jesus, remember me when Thou comest in Thy Kingdom." The enemy of God had become, through the reconciliation of Christ, the friend of God. That must be forever a picture of what Christ does for the soul of man.

Nothing but the Cross could bring about this reconciliation between man and God. Death sometimes has had reconciling effect. I have seen members of families who were alienated reconciled by a death which came into the family circle. When Abraham died, his sons, Isaac and Ishmael forgot their feud, and buried him in the Cave of Machpelah. A father and son who had become bitter enemies were brought together by the bedside of the dying wife and mother. The dying woman took the hand of her son and placed it in the hand of her husband. Thus death reconciled father and son. The death of Christ, the greatest act of God's love and mercy, reconciles God and man. With arms outstretched on the Cross, Christ lays hold upon man and brings him to God.

Only the Cross can sound the depths of the human heart. We have peace through the Cross. Only the Cross can take away the stain of sin and the guilt of sin. Only the Cross can still the tempest of conscience.

God is the Author of the great Armistice which was signed by Christ on the Cross. But it is man who receives it and benefits by it. It takes two to make a covenant, or sign an armistice. When the agreement is signed, then there is peace. If either of the belligerent parties had refused to sign the armistice on that November day in 1918, there would have been no peace. Christ as His ambassador signed it in the blood of the Cross. When by faith and repentance you also sign it, then there is peace. Heaven's banners are flung out and there is joy in heaven over the peace which has come to a soul, for Christ would have come and died on the Cross had there been just one soul at war with God. Whenever by his repentance and his faith man accepts the peace offered him by God, then God withdraws the armies of His condemnation and His Judgment. Henceforth, therefore, there is no more condemnation to them that are in Christ Jesus.

This is the heart of the Gospel, the heart of Christianity, that Christ has made peace by the blood of His Cross; and all else is but the illustration, the expression, or the application of it.

Acquaint now thyself with God and be at peace with Him. Are you at peace with God? That does not mean: Are you satisfied with yourself? Are you enjoying life? Are you having reasonable success? All that may be true, and still you may be at war with God. Are you at peace with God? Have you accepted His terms? Have you signed the armistice? There is your Saviour's Name written for you in crimson colors of the Cross. Therefore, I beseech you, "Be ye reconciled unto God." When we answer the invitation of God's love and mercy, when we accept the pardon which Christ holds out to us with His pierced hand, then there is peace, peace with God, peace with the world, peace with ourselves. This is the peace about which Christ was speaking when He said, "My peace I give unto you."

It is the peace which the world cannot give, and which the world cannot take away.

Citizens of the Kingdom

The Sermon on the Mount is the King's manifesto of His kingdom principles, as taught by our coming King. When the King delivered this, the greatest of all sermons, His words must have been strange in the ears of His disciples, and amazing to the listening multitudes.

Many believed that John the Baptist was the forerunner of the Messiah. They had heard him declare, "I am the voice of one crying in the wilderness: Make straight the way of the LORD, as the prophet Isaiah said" (John 1:23; also Is. 40:3). To prepare the way for the coming of the King, John preached repentance. He said, "Repent, for the kingdom of heaven is at hand!" (Matt. 3:2). After the Lord's baptism by John (in the river Jordan), His temptation in the wilderness, and the imprisonment of John the Baptist, Jesus began His public ministry (Mark 1:14, 15). He preached repentance, saying, "Repent, for the kingdom of heaven is at hand" (Matt. 4:17). The King could not set up His kingdom on earth because Israel would not repent and believe the good news of the kingdom.

John the apostle said, "He came to His own [Israel], and His own did not receive Him. But as many as received Him, to them He gave the right to become children of God, to those who believe in His name" (John 1:11, 12). Some did repent and receive Him by faith, as their Messiah. But the leaders of Israel, and the Romans, nailed Him to the cross. Jesus, knowing that He was to die for the sins of the world, promised to come again and establish God's kingdom on earth, and to sit on the throne of His glory (Matt. 25:31), which is the throne of His father David, according to the flesh.

God made an unconditional promise to King David when He said, "I will set upon your throne the fruit [descendants] of your body" (Ps. 132:11). God promised King David the He would be born of His descending line according to the flesh (Rom. 1:3). He, the God-Man, would be seated on the throne of David (Acts 2:30; cf. Is. 9:6, 7).

We do not have the kingdom of heaven on earth, but we do have the King's manifesto. Even though we are not living in the kingdom, we are to practice kingdom life in this corrupt world system. The Beatitudes reveal the secret of true happiness. Study them with an open heart, a receptive mind, and a humble spirit, praying always. Remember that happiness is not found in the things you have, but in what you are in Christ Jesus. "Therefore, if anyone is in Christ, he is a new creation; old things have passed away; behold, all things have become new" (2 Cor. 5:17). In this verse we have old things and new things. The old things are the fruits of man (1 Cor. 2:14); the new things are the fruits of the new man in Christ.

> The Poor in Spirit
> (Matthew 5:1-3)
> The Mourners
> (Matthew 5:4)
> The Meek
> (Matthew 5:5)
> The Hungry and Thirsty
> (Matthew 5:6)
> The Merciful
> (Matthew 5:7)
> The Pure in Heart
> (Matthew 5:8)
> The Peacemakers
> (Matthew 5:9)
> The Persecuted
> (Matthew 5:10-12)

The Poor in Spirit (Matthew 5:1-3)

"Blessed are the poor in spirit, for theirs is the kingdom of heaven" (v. 3). The poor in spirit are empty of all spiritual pride; they know that spiritual pride is the spirit of this age of which Satan is god (2 Cor. 4:4).

To be poor in spirit is to have "a contrite and humble spirit" (Is. 57:15)—to be conscious of your unworthiness. Peter demonstrated this quality when he fell at the knees of Jesus, saying, "Depart from me, for I am a sinful man, O Lord" (Luke 5:1-11). The Pharisee of the parable boasted in his religious pride, but the contrite and humble tax collector was truly "poor in spirit" (Luke 18:9-14).

The Mourners (Matthew 5:1-3)—"Blessed are those who mourn, for they shall be comforted" (v. 4). This paradoxical beatitude can be understood only by the believer. How can a bereaved person be blessed amid grief? Because he knows that "weeping may endure for a night, but joy comes in the morning" (Ps. 30:5), that God has promised to comfort the mourner in this life and in the life to come. Heaven's joys will abundantly compensate for earth's sorrows.

We should also mourn for lost souls. Paul grieved for his "countrymen according to the flesh," and longed desperately for their salvation (Rom. 9:1-5). Some lost souls lament their life of sin when they repent and believe on the Lord Jesus Christ as their personal Savior. The penitent publican "beat his breast, saying, 'God be merciful to me a sinner'" (Luke 18:13). Mourning is a part of true repentance

The Meek (Matthew 5:5)—"Blessed are the meek [gentle], for they shall inherit the earth" (v. 5; also Ps. 37:11). The philosophy of the world is the exact opposite of this beatitude. People of the world consider the meek person to be weak and cowardly, a Caspar Milquetoast to be treated with contempt. The most gentle, meek, humble person that ever lived on this earth was the Lord Jesus Christ, who said, "I am gentle and lowly [humble] in heart, and you [that come to Me] will find rest for your souls" (Matt. 11:28-30). This gentle Son of God entered the temple as the Jews were preparing for the Passover and the Feast of Unleavened Bread (Ex. 12:1-51). He overturned the tables of the moneychangers, and with a whip of cords He drove out those who sold oxen, sheep, and doves in the sanctity of the temple. He said, "Do not make My Father's house a house of merchandise" (John 2:13-16). Was this the act of a weak and cowardly man? Yet He is the Man who said, "Blessed are the meek, for they shall inherit the earth" (v. 5).

To know the characteristics of a truly meek (gentle) person, study this passage: "Therefore I ask that you do not lose heart at my tribulations for you, which is your glory. For this reason I bow my knees to the Father of our Lord Jesus Christ, from whom the whole family in heaven and earth is named, that He would grant you, according to the riches of His glory, to be strengthened with might through His Spirit in the inner man, that Christ may dwell in your hearts through faith; that you, being rooted and grounded in love, may be able to comprehend with all the saints what is the width and length and depth and height—to know the love of Christ which passes knowledge; that you may be filled with all the fullness of God" (Eph. 3:13-19).

No, the meek are not weak; they are "strong in the Lord and in the power of His might" (Eph. 6:10)!

The Hungry and Thirsty (Matthew 5:6)—"Blessed are those who hunger and thirst for righteousness, for they shall be filled" (v. 6). We have often heard it said that the world is hungry for the gospel of the grace of God. But if this were so, the whole world would be saved in a very short time. The truth is that people of the world hunger and thirst, not for righteousness, but to satisfy the lust of the flesh, the lust of the eyes, and the pride of life (1 John 2:16, 17). This yields no lasting happiness. By faith Moses chose to suffer affliction alongside God's people, rather than enjoy the passing happiness and fleeting pleasures of sin. The happiness of sin is short-lived, but the happiness of the godly life is eternal (Heb. 11:23-29).

The Scriptures describe two kinds of righteousness:

(1) Legal or self-righteousness, which is man's vain effort to establish his own righteousness by his own works—works of the law (Rom. 10:1-3). Such "law works" cannot save (Titus 3:5; Eph. 2:8, 9); they produce only self-righteousness, which in the sight of God is "filthy rags" (Is. 64:6).

(2) The righteousness of God in Christ. "For Christ is the end of the law for righteousness to everyone who believes" (Rom. 10:4). Faith alone brings lasting happiness. "For with the heart one believes unto righteousness, and with the mouth confession is made unto salvation" (Rom. 10:10). Believers live the righteous life, but they do so not in order to be saved, but because they know they are saved. Happiness is salvation's reward. In this life there is no greater joy. And there is even better to come: John said, "We know that when He is revealed [when Jesus comes again], we shall be like Him, for we shall see Him as He is" (1 John 3:2). We shall see Him in all His glory. This will be heavenly happiness.

The Merciful (Matthew 5:7)—"Blessed are the merciful, for they shall obtain mercy" (v. 7). This beatitude does not mean that, if you show mercy to people, they in turn will show mercy to you. Some will, but not all; some may even persecute you in return. We cannot expect to receive mercy from those who do not know our merciful Savior. Jesus Christ showed mercy throughout His earthly ministry. He healed the sick, He cleansed the lepers, and He made the dumb speak, the deaf hear, the blind see, and the lame walk. He raised the dead and fed the multitudes. He never failed to show mercy, but did He obtain mercy from the people?

We are to show mercy, knowing well that the recipient may never show mercy in return. We are to bestow it in the name of our merciful Christ, who Himself will reward us in this life and in heaven. An illustration is the parable of the Good Samaritan, spoken by Jesus in answer to a lawyer who asked, "And who is my neighbor?" (Luke 10:29). Jesus told a man traveling from Jerusalem to Jericho who was robbed, wounded, and left half dead by thieves. A priest came by and saw the man, but did not stop to help; he showed no mercy. A Levite also came along, stopped to look, then continued on his journey; he showed no mercy. But a Samaritan saw him, had compassion on him, and helped him without expecting anything in return. Jesus asked the lawyer, "So which of these three do you think was neighbor to him who fell among the thieves?" When the lawyer answered, "He who showed mercy on him, "Jesus said, "Go and do likewise" (Luke 10:25-37). "Blessed are the merciful, for they shall obtain mercy."

The Pure in Heart (Matthew 5:8)—"Blessed are the pure in heart, for they shall see God" (v. 8). The unsaved man cannot have a pure heart as long as he rejects the Lord Jesus as his Savior (Acts 4:12); the things of God are foolishness to him (1 Cor. 2:14). The natural (unregenerate) heart is deceitful above all things and desperately wicked (Jer. 17:9).

Who are the pure in heart?

(1) They are void of hypocrisy (Ps. 24:3-5).
(2) They have room for only one master, Christ (Matt. 6:24).
(3) They thirst for God as a deer thirsts for the water brook (Ps. 42:1).
(4) They have a newly created heart (2 Cor. 5:17). David prayed, "Create in me a clean heart, O God" (Ps. 51:10).
(5) They confess and forsake all known sin (Prov. 28:13).
(6) They never try to hide sin from God (Ps. 32:5).
(7) They are able to sin but cannot be happy in sin (Ps. 51:1-4). When they sin, they repent and seek forgiveness (1 John 1:9).
(8) They are spiritually minded; they have the mind of Christ (1 Cor. 2:15, 16).

Only they will see God.

The Peacemakers (Matthew 5:9)—"Blessed are the peacemakers, for they shall be called sons of God" (v. 9). To become this kind of peacemaker, we must first be "justified freely by His grace through the redemption that is in Christ Jesus" (Rom. 3:24). To be justified is to be declared just by almighty God because of the imputed righteousness of the Lord Jesus Christ. For God to declare us just, we must believe that

(1) Christ was offered on the cross to bear our sins (Heb. 9:28);
(2) He was buried in the tomb three days and nights;
(3) He rose again the third day according to the Scriptures (1 Cor. 15:3, 4).

"Therefore, having been justified by faith, we have peace with God through our Lord Jesus Christ" (Rom. 5:1). Now that we have peace with God, we can also share our faith with those at enmity against God (Rom. 8:7, 8). A peacemaker is one who shares the gospel with those who are lost, showing them how they can have peace with God, after being justified by grace through faith in the Lord Jesus Christ (Eph. 2:8, 9).

The Persecuted (Matthew 5:10-12)—"Blessed are those who are persecuted for righteousness' sake, for theirs is the kingdom of heaven" (vv. 10-12). This is a beautiful and vivid description of mature Christians. They are reviled and persecuted because they love the Lord Jesus Christ, and have been given the righteousness of God. How do mature Christians respond to such persecution? They rejoice and are exceedingly glad, because they know the speeches against them are lies. They also know that a great reward awaits them in heaven.

Persecution harassed the church from the start. The apostles were arrested and tried before the Sanhedrin for preaching Christ and for doing many miracles in His name. Some wanted to put them to death, and even though Gamaliel persuaded the Sanhedrin to let them go, they were beaten before their release.

But this did not stop them from preaching the gospel. "They departed from the presence of the council, rejoicing that they were counted worthy to suffer shame for His name" (Acts 5:33-42).

Believers Are Salt and Light (Matthew 5:13-16)—Believers are salt and light (vv. 13-16). The teachings of Jesus are rich in parabolic metaphors. In these verses, He uses two familiar and important elements of everyday life: salt and light.

Enoch, a Man Who Walked with God

The biography of Enoch is brief, only nine verses in all: five verses in Genesis, two in Hebrews, and two in Jude. Yet this remarkable biography points the Bible student to a man who was unique among all men of all generations. For three hundred years Enoch put God first in his life. The Lord was preeminent in everything: in his thinking, in his ways, and in his walk. He was first in his love, in his service, and the only One whom he worshiped. Following are some of the ways in which Enoch was unique:

(1) He was one of two men whom the Scripture says that he "walked with God." The other was Noah (Gen. 6:9). We are not told how long Noah walked with God; however, we are told that Enoch "walked with God three hundred years" (Gen. 5:22).

(2) He was the first of two men who were taken to heaven without experiencing physical death. Elijah was the other (2 Kin. 2:11).

(3) Enoch was the seventh generation from Adam. Of all the generations before Enoch we read, "And he died;" but with Enoch it was changed, for we read, "And he was not, for God took him" (Gen. 5:24).

(4) He became the father of the oldest man who ever lived, Methuselah, who lived 969 years (Gen. 5:21).

(5) He walked with God three hundred years. During those years he was a family man; he was the father of sons and daughters.

(6) Enoch was justified by faith; therefore he lived by faith (Heb. 10:38).

(7) Enoch prophesied that the Lord would come and execute judgment on the ungodly (Jude 14, 15).

The remainder of the biography of Enoch will not be known until we, too, put on immortality and continue our walk with God in eternity.

Enoch Walked with God
(Genesis 5:21-23)
Enoch Walked by Faith with God
(Hebrews 11:5, 6)
Enoch Walked Humbly with God
(Micah 6:8)
Enoch Walked in Agreement with God
(Amos 3:3)

Enoch Walked with God (Genesis 5:21-23)—"Enoch walked with God three hundred years" (v. 22). One day, as they walked together, it was as though the Lord said, "Enoch, come home and let us continue our walk in heaven." This is the way it might have happened for the Scripture says, "Enoch walked with God; and he was not, for God took him" (v. 24). Enoch continued his "walk with God" in glory, a walk that will never end. And all this began when, one day during his life on earth, Enoch got in step with God, walking with Him for three hundred years thereafter, without interruption.

(1) To walk with God requires five things:

    a. *Righteousness.* This is not self-righteousness, which Isaiah calls "filthy rags" (Is. 64:6), but the imputed righteousness of God (Rom. 10:1-4). Enoch was a righteous man, "strong in the Lord and in the power of His might" (Eph. 6:10). He was "like a tree planted by the river of water" (Ps. 1:3), rooted and grounded in the truth (John 8:32). "The LORD knows the way of the righteous" (Ps. 1:6), because they walk with Him in righteousness. But it is not so with the ungodly. They cannot walk with God; they are unstable in all their ways; they are like chaff in a windstorm, driven about by the doctrines of this world system, which are promulgated by the servants of Satan (John 8:44; 2 Cor. 4:4).

    b. *Faith.* Faith is required in the fact that God does exist and that He is the sovereign, almighty, eternal God. "For he who comes to God must believe that He is, and that He is a rewarder of those who diligently seek Him" (Heb. 11:6). Enoch sought the Lord by faith, found Him, and walked with Him by faith (Rom. 1:17).

(2) *Uprightness.* Enoch was governed by high moral principles and adhered to all the virtues of a true believer. "For the LORD God is a sun and shield; the LORD will give grace and glory; no good thing will He withhold from those who walk uprightly" (Ps. 84:11). Enoch walked with God uprightly and lived life abundantly (John 10:10).

(3) *Humility.* A truly humble person will not be afflicted with that common disease known as "inflated ego." John the Baptist said of Jesus, "He must increase, but I must decrease" (John 3:30). When you walk with God, the "I" (ego) will diminish to its proper limits and then the words of Paul will be understood: "If anyone thinks himself to be something, when he is nothing, he deceives himself" (Gal. 6:3).

(4) *Commitment.* Total commitment is called for. This means that the whole person—spirit, soul, and body—is placed figuratively on the altar of God as a burnt sacrifice (a burnt sacrifice was completely consumed by fire). You are to be a "living sacrifice . . . that you may prove what is that good and acceptable and perfect will of God" (Rom. 12:1, 2). Enoch knew what it meant to commit his way to the Lord (Ps. 37:5).

(5) When you walk with God:

    a.   You will "fear no evil," even when He leads you through "the valley of the shadow of death" (Ps. 23:4). You will not be afraid, because you know that He is with you, and that His grace is sufficient for all of life's events (2 Cor. 12:9).

    b.   You will never walk in darkness, because "God is light and in Him is no darkness at all . . . if we walk in the light as He is in the light, we have fellowship with one another" (1 John 1:5-7). When we walk with God, as Enoch did, we have fellowship with the Father, Son, and Holy Spirit—and all the saints of God who are walking with Him. This is heavenly fellowship, and it is forever and ever.

(6) "If you abide in My word, you are My disciples indeed. And you shall know the truth, and the truth shall make you free" (John 8:31, 32). The Truth that sets you free is the Lord Jesus Christ (John 14:6). To walk with God is to walk with the Lord Jesus Christ, who is the Living Word. John said, "The Word was with God, and the Word was God" (John 1:1). Enoch walked with the Living Word.

Enoch Walked All the Way to Heaven with God (Genesis 5:24)—
"Enoch walked with God; and he was not, for God took him" (v. 24). This
verse says three things about Enoch that deserve our attention. Each statement
is brief, direct, simple, and yet profound. To discover the depth of this verse
and the riches of its simplicity, we go to the New Testament.

a.   "Enoch walked with God." As he walked by faith "he had this
       testimony, that he pleased God" (Heb. 11:5). Enoch's walk
       with God was no secret; all who knew him must have said,
       "There goes a man who pleases God." He prophesied the
       second coming of Christ, and the judgments of God upon
       the ungodly in the last days (Jude 14, 15). First, he lived his
       testimony; and second, he preached the good news of the
       coming of the Lord. What is meant when it is said that Enoch
       walked with God by faith?

(a) It means that he got in step with God, and made spiritual progress one
    step at a time; he grew in the grace and knowledge of God (2 Pet. 3:17,
    18). He was steadfast in his walk with God, all the way to heaven.
(b) It means that he could no longer go in his own way (Is. 53:6), or walk
    according to the course of this world system, which is satanic (Eph.
    2:1, 2). If he would walk with God, he must seek God's way and walk
    in it (Matt. 6:33).
(c) It implies total commitment to the revealed will of God (Rom. 12:1, 2).
    Enoch's life demonstrates the good and perfect will of God. He could
    say with David, "I delight to do Your will, O my God" (Ps. 40:8).

b.   "Enoch walked with God; and he was not." One day Enoch
       vanished, disappeared, and was taken up into heaven in
       the presence of witnesses. When Elijah was taken up in a
       whirlwind, Elisha witnessed his translation (2 Kin. 2:1-13).
       When Jesus was taken up, the disciples were witnesses (Acts
       1:9-11). Enoch had his ungodly critics, as does anyone who
       walks with God. Because of them, had there been no witnesses
       when he was translated, there would probably have been no
       record of his translation. Further proof of witnesses is found
       in the New Testament. "By faith Enoch was taken away so
       that he did not see death, 'and was not found'" (Heb. 11:5).
       Unbelievers may have searched for him to prove that his

translation was a religious hoax. When Elisha brought word to the school of the prophets that Elijah had been translated, they doubted Elisha and formed search parties and looked in vain for him. People searched for Enoch, but he "was not found, because God had taken him."

c.   "Enoch walked with God; and he was not, for God took him." Again we go to the New Testament for a better understanding of this brief and beautiful statement, "for God took him." And we read, "By faith Enoch was taken away so that he did not see death" (Heb. 11:5). His spirit and soul were not separated from his body of flesh. Had he died physically, his spirit and soul would have left his body, and search parties could have found it and buried it. Enoch was taken up (translated) because he pleased God by faith. Now all who please God by faith will be resurrected and caught up like Enoch at the Rapture, and will be given glorified bodies (1 Thess. 4:16, 17). "Amen. Even so, come, Lord Jesus!" (Rev. 22:20).

Enoch Walked by Faith with God (Hebrews 11:5, 6)—God's Word reveals seven things that Enoch did by faith:

(1)   By faith Enoch walked with God three hundred years. His faith must have been tested and tried many times. But there is no evidence that he ever lowered the "shield of faith," with which he was able to quench all of Satan's fiery darts (Eph. 6:16).

(2)   By faith Enoch was "taken away," that is, taken up to heaven—body, soul, and spirit. And his body of flesh was glorified because "flesh and blood cannot inherit the kingdom of God" (1 Cor. 15:50-55).

(3)   By faith Enoch "did not see death" (v. 5). Enoch is a type of all born-again believers who will be alive when Jesus comes back to this world. The dead in Christ will be resurrected, and the living will be caught up with the resurrected saints to meet the Lord in the air (1 Thess. 4:13-18).

(4)   By faith Enoch pleased God. Because Enoch walked with God by faith, all who knew him knew that he pleased God. "He had this testimony, that he pleased God" (v. 5). Enoch had faith that could be seen by all who knew him—by the

way he talked, lived, and worked. Faith can be seen in our manner of life.

Jesus was teaching in a house in Capernaum, and four men brought a paralytic to Him. When they could not enter (because the house was filled with people), they went up on top of the house, removed a section of the roof, and let the man down on his bed before Jesus. And the Scripture says, "When Jesus saw their faith" He forgave the sins of the paralytic and healed him (Mark 2:1-5). Can your loved ones, friends, neighbors, and acquaintances see the proof of your faith?

(5) By faith Enoch believed that Almighty God did exist. "For he who comes to God must believe that He is" (v. 6). Where did Enoch get such great faith? He did not have the Bible or any books of the Bible. God must have manifested Himself to Enoch, as He did to others, before the Son, the Lord Jesus Christ, became a man. Enoch had an ever-present witness of God.

"The heavens declare the glory of God; and the firmament shows His handwork. Day unto day utters speech, and night unto night reveals knowledge" (Ps. 19: 1, 2). Creation reveals the glory of the Creator, day and night. When Enoch looked at God's creation, he saw more than the sun, moon, and stars. He saw more than mountains, valleys, rivers, lakes, streams, and seas. He saw more than trees, flowers, the birds of the air, the beasts of the fields, the fish of the sea, or man who was created in the image of God. Enoch, by faith, saw the reflection of the Creator in His creation. He sought the Creator God, and found Him, because he sought Him with his whole heart (Ps. 119:2).

(6) By faith Enoch was rewarded. He was not rewarded with eternal life, because eternal life is God's gift; it cannot be earned (Eph. 2:8, 9). God rewarded Enoch by allowing him to walk with Himself.

(7) By faith Enoch diligently sought God. We do not know how long he sought Him before God invited Enoch to walk with Him; it could have been sixty-five years. The years of seeking were years of growing. As he sought God one day, his growth in grace and knowledge was sufficient, and he walked by faith into the very heavenly presence of God.

Enoch Walked Humbly with God (Micah 6:8)—All who walk with God are required to "walk humbly" (v. 8) with Him. We know that Enoch was a humble man, because he "walked with God three hundred years" (Gen. 5:22). To understand true humility we must know some of the characteristics of a humble person.

d.   He is gentle, but never weak. Jesus said of Himself, "I am gentle and lowly in heart" (Matt. 11:29). He was the most meek person this world will ever know—yet He once took a whip and drove the moneychangers from the temple (John 2:13-16). This was not the act of a weak man.

e.   He is bold for the Lord, but never brazen. "Now when they [the Sanhedrin] saw the boldness of Peter and John, and perceived that they were uneducated and untrained men, they marveled. And they realized that they had been with Jesus" (Acts 4:1-22). Peter and John were bold because they had accompanied Jesus for three years, and had witnessed His death, burial, and resurrection.

f.   He is aggressive for the Lord, but never contentious or hostile. The apostles never held back with the gospel of Jesus Christ, even though the Sanhedrin warned them, "Did we not strictly command you not to teach in this name? And look, you have filled Jerusalem with your doctrine, and intend to bring this Man's blood on us!" (Acts 5:22-32).

g.   He is poor in spirit, but never spiritually poor (Matt. 5:3). The poor in spirit never think more highly of themselves than they ought (Rom. 12:3). They believe themselves to be a new creation in Christ, knowing that "old things have passed away; behold, all things have become new" (2 Cor. 5:17). The poor in spirit know that before honor can come their way, they must walk humbly with God (v. 8), who gives to the humble preference and honor among those in Christ. There is no room for arrogance, pride, or jealousy in the heart or mind of the person who walks humbly with God (Prov. 15:33).

Enoch Walked in Agreement with God (Amos 3:3)—"Can two walk together, unless they are agreed?" (v. 3). Enoch walked in agreement with God for three hundred years, continuously conforming his life to the counsel of God. He must have learned that "the LORD brings the counsel of the nations to nothing . . . [but] the counsel of the LORD stands forever" (Ps. 33:10, 11). Enoch chose to walk into eternity with the infinite God; and as he traveled, he was guided by God's counsel day after day until he was translated into His heavenly presence (Ps. 73:24). Enoch had a choice, to walk in agreement with God, or to walk in the counsel of the ungodly (Ps. 1:1).

God gave Judah a choice before He sent them into seventy years of captivity: "'Come now, and let us reason together,' says the LORD, 'Though your sins are like scarlet, they shall be as white as snow; though they are red like crimson, they shall be as wool'" (Is. 1:18). Judah was out of step with God, its people walking in the counsel of the ungodly. When they refused to walk with Him, He sent them into captivity. Every nation and individual has this choice: they can walk in agreement with God, as Enoch did, or walk in the way that seems right to man, though the end of the walk that seems right to man is eternal separation from God (Prov. 14:12).

Enoch began his walk with God in the year that Methuselah was born (Gen. 5:21, 22). For three hundred years Enoch walked in faith, and in agreement with God.

Entering the Kingdom

In the fourth and concluding section of the King's manifesto, we have the Golden Rule, the key that unlocks the treasure chest of the Sermon on the Mount. It is the essence of His kingdom principles. "Therefore, whatever you want men to do to you, do also to them, for this is the Law and the Prophets" (Matt. 7:12). Jesus was saying that when you practice the Golden Rule, you are fulfilling the Law and the Prophets.

On a later occasion, a certain lawyer tested Jesus by asking Him this question, "Teacher, which is the great commandment in the law?" (Matt. 22:36). Jesus knew that the intent of the lawyer was to trap Him and destroy his influence with the masses. He had taught earlier in His ministry, "Do not think that I came to destroy the Law or the Prophets. I did not come to destroy but to fulfill" (Matt. 5:17). Had Jesus named any one of the laws as the greatest, He would have degraded the other nine commandments. They could then have accused Him of being an unreliable teacher of the law. However, they were not ready for His answer. He did not name just one law as the greatest, but He divided the ten laws into two sections and answered them by saying, 'You shall love the LORD your God with all your heart, with all your soul, and with all your mind.' This is the first and great commandment" (Matt. 22:37, 38). He then went on to say, "And the second is like it: 'You shall love your neighbor as yourself.' On these two commandments hang all the Law and the Prophets" (Matt. 22:39, 40).

When you love God with all your heart, all your soul, and all your mind, you are obeying the first four of the ten commandments; and when you love your neighbor as yourself, you are obeying the last six of the ten commandments (Ex. 20:1-17). When you reach that spiritual plateau where you truly love your neighbor as you love yourself, you are practicing the Golden Rule. It will be a joy, day after day, to do unto others as you would have others do unto you (Matt. 7:12).

At the conclusion of the King's manifesto, the multitudes were astonished at His teaching; it is no wonder that they were amazed, for He taught them as one having authority (Matt. 7:28, 29). He contradicted almost all the traditional interpretations of the scribes and Pharisees, while in His life and teaching He fulfilled all the Law and the Prophets:

> Prayer is Asking, Seeking and Knocking
> (Matt. 7:7-11)
> The Key to the Kingdom
> (Matt. 7:12)
> Two Ways: The Broad and the Narrow
> (Matt. 7:13, 14)
> Two Prophets: The False and the True
> (Matt. 7:15-20)
> Religious but Lost
> (Matt. 7:21-23)
> Two Builders: The Wise and the Foolish
> (Matt. 7:24-27)
> Two Authorities: Sovereign and Human
> (Matt. 7:28, 29)

Fear

The subject of fear is one of the most awesome studies in God's Word. There are constructive and destructive fears. Some fears are so evil that one can be momentarily paralyzed by them. One can become physically ill through fear. Therefore, it is so important that we give ourselves over to the Lord as we study this important subject. All of the spiritual qualifications and tools necessary to combat the evil fears that may come upon us are found in the Word of God. We can overcome bad fears, be victorious, live happy and joyful Christian lives, and be of greater service and value to our Master.

The following are fears that can keep us from knowing the Lord and doing His will, and that may condemn some to eternal hell:

(1) The fear that you will fail;
(2) The fear that you can't live up to God's standards;
(3) The fear that you can't obey God's Word.

Forms of the words *fear* and *afraid* are found over seven hundred times in the Bible; this should cause us to realize the importance of fear in our lives. Over eighty times we have the words, "Do not fear," or "Fear not."

Fear, Constructive and Destructive
(Matthew 10:24-31)
Fear, Godly
(Psalm 33:8)
Fear Not: God Is Your Protector
(Genesis 15:1)
Fear Not: God Is Your Power
(2 Kings 6:16)

Fear: Its Objects
(Psalm 34:4)

Fear, Constructive and Destructive (Matthew 10:24-31)—Jesus said to His fearful disciples, "And do not fear those who kill the body but cannot kill the soul" (v. 28). This is *destructive* fear. Jesus warned them that they would be persecuted for preaching the gospel, and would have no physical defense. He said, "Behold, I send you out as sheep in the midst of wolves" (vv. 16-23). The apostles suffered severe persecution; indeed, nearly all the apostles were put to death. They could have denied their faith and lived—but they refused.

Consider these five great Biblical saints who trusted God and overcame fear, even in the face of death:

(1) Moses chose "rather to suffer affliction with the people of God than to enjoy the passing pleasures of sin . . . By faith he forsook Egypt, not fearing the wrath of the king" (Heb. 11:25-27).

(2) The three Hebrew children, because of their faith, were unafraid of Nebuchadnezzar and his fiery furnace (Dan. 3:16-18).

(3) Daniel was not afraid of the decree of King Darius and the den of lions. By faith he defied the king's command, knowing that he would be cast into a den of hungry lions. Like his three Hebrew friends, he was courageous (Dan. 6:1-28).

(4) Stephen, one of the first deacons, "full of faith and power, did great wonders and signs among the people" (Acts 6:8). He was the first Christian to suffer a martyr's death for exalting Christ. Stephen died on his knees, stoned by the enemies of Jesus. Unafraid, he prayed, "Lord, do not charge them with this sin" (Acts 7:54-60).

(5) Paul wrote to young Timothy from Rome about his own coming death: "For I am already being poured out as a drink offering, and the time of my departure is at hand. I have fought the good fight, I have finished the race, I have kept the faith" (2 Tim. 4:6, 7). In his letter to the church at Philippi, he said, "For to me to live is Christ, and to die is gain" (Phil. 1:21). By faith Paul was not afraid of death; to him it would be eternal gain.

There are two elements that will deliver you from destructive fear, whether fear of death or life, fear of failure or loss, fear of people or position, or fear of rank or power. These elements are

(1) *Faith.* You cannot trust God and be fearful at the same time. The psalmist said, "Whenever I am afraid, I will trust in You. In God (I will praise His word), in God I have put my trust; I will not fear. What can flesh do to me?" (Ps. 56:3, 4). Sudden fear gripped the psalmist for a moment, then he cried, "Whenever I am afraid . . ." At the moment fear grips you, turn to God in faith. The psalmist went on to say, "I will trust in You." When faith came to him, he was able to say, "I will not fear. What can flesh do to me?" You cannot truly trust God and worry.

Paul tells us to take "the shield of faith with which you will be able to quench all the fiery darts of the wicked one" (Eph. 6:16) and that ability is there the moment you lift up the shield. Fear is one of Satan's fiery darts. The shield of faith will extinguish it.

(2) *Love.* "There is no fear in love; but perfect love casts out fear" (1 John 4:18). There is but one perfect love—the love of God. Let the Holy Spirit fill your heart with God's perfect love and there will be no room for destructive fear (Rom. 5:5).

With your faith in God and your heart filled with His love, you are equipped with the two elements necessary to give you victory over all destructive fear.

Now let us examine constructive or reverential fear. "But rather fear Him who is able to destroy both soul and body in hell" (v. 28). Some believe Jesus is telling us here that Satan does not have this kind of power. Only God has the power and right to cast both soul and body into hell. Satan is a defeated foe. James urges us to "submit to God. Resist the devil and he will flee from you" (James 4:7). When our lives are committed to God, we can resist Satan by faith, actually causing him to flee from us. We are to fear our holy God with a reverential fear—fear that bows in awe as we worship and praise Him. Remember, "There is no [destructive] fear in love" (1 John 4:18). Perfect love produces reverential fear. We are to worship, praise, and exalt God in holy fear.

Fear, Godly (Psalm 33:8)—"Let all the earth fear the Lord" (v.8). All the earth will fear the Lord in His coming kingdom. Till then we thank God for those who fear Him in the sin-sick world (Rom. 3:18). Let us remember:

(1) The fear of the Lord is the beginning of knowledge and wisdom (Prov. 1:7; 15:33).
(2) The fear of the Lord is godly fear (Heb. 12:28).
(3) The fear of the Lord is righteous fear, "He loves righteousness" (Ps. 33:5).
(4) The fear of the Lord is holy fear (2 Cor. 7:1).
(5) The fear of the Lord is reverential fear (Heb. 12:28).
(6) The fear of the Lord is to stand in awe of Him. "Let all the inhabitants of the world stand in awe of Him" (Ps. 33:8).
(7) To fear the Lord is to worship Him in spirit and truth (John 4:24).
(8) To fear the Lord is to "serve God acceptably with reverence and godly fear" (Heb. 12:28).

Godly fear brings joy. The psalmist said, "Rejoice in the Lord, O you righteous! . . . Praise the Lord with the harp . . . Sing to Him a new song" (Ps. 33:1-3). Speaking of joy, the apostle John said, "These things we write to you that your joy may be full. This is the message . . . that God is light" (1 John 1:4, 5).

Is there godly fear in your heart? To be sure that you have godly fear, examine the following verses in 1 John 1:6-10.

(1) "If we [who say we are believers] say that we have fellowship with Him [the Lord Jesus Christ], and walk in darkness [live in known, unconfessed sin], we lie, and do not practice the truth" (1 John 1:6, cf. Acts 5:1-4).
(2) "But if we walk in the light as He is in the light, we have fellowship with one another [we have fellowship with God because we are in His light—His righteousness], and the blood of Jesus Christ His Son cleanse us from all sin" (1 John 1:7, cf. Rev. 1:5). Godly fear can be known only by those who have been cleansed by the precious blood of Jesus (1 Pet. 1:18, 19).
(3) "If we say that we have no sin, we deceive ourselves, and the truth is not in us" (1 John 1:8, cf. Gal. 6:7, 8).
(4) "If we confess our sins, He is faithful and just to forgive us our sins and to cleanse us from all unrighteousness" (1 John 1:9). To be cleansed by the blood brings the lost or unsaved into a relationship with God the Father. To be cleansed from sins which you commit after you are born into the family of God, you must confess them to our Lord, calling each

known sin by name. Godly fear will cause you to search your heart every time you go to God in prayer; and if you find any unconfessed sin in your heart, however small, judge it, confess it, and forsake it. Practice 1 John 1:9 every day, and thus stay in fellowship with the Lord.

(5) "If we say that we have not sinned, we make Him a liar, and His Word is not in us" (1 John 1:10). Godly fear will not let you say, "I have no sin," or "I cannot sin in the flesh," or "I have not sinned since the Lord saved me." Yet godly fear can also help you to resist temptation (1 Cor. 10:13).

"My little children, these things I write to you, so that you may not sin. And if anyone sins, we have an Advocate with the Father, Jesus Christ the righteous" (1 John 2:1).

Fear: Its Objects (Psalm 34:4)—The following are some of the objects of fear:

(1) *Manifestations of Deity.* When John was exiled to the island of Patmos, he was visited by the risen glorified Christ (Rev. 1:12-17). John records that "I fell at His feet as dead," but Jesus reassured him, saying, "Do not be afraid." See Daniel 8:15-17 for a similar visitation of the Lord.

(2) Manifestations of angels.

    (a) The aged priest Zacharias and his wife Elizabeth had no children (Elizabeth was barren), but longed and prayed for a child. One day, as Zacharias was burning incense in the temple, an angel of the Lord appeared to him. When he saw the angel, Zacharias was gripped by fear (Luke 1:5-25).

    (b) When Jesus was born in Bethlehem, the shepherds were keeping watch over their flocks: "And behold, an angel of the Lord stood before them, and the glory of the Lord shone around them, and they were greatly afraid" (Luke 2:9).

    (c) As the Roman soldiers guarded the tomb of Jesus, "an angel of the Lord descended from heaven, and came and rolled back the stone from the door, and say on it . . . And the guards shook for fear of him, and became like dead men" (Matt. 28:1-4). They were momentarily petrified with fear.

(3) *Fear of meeting God in our sins.* The first mention of fear in the Bible is in Genesis 3, when Adam and Eve sinned in the Garden of Eden. The Word says, "The eyes of both of them were opened, and they knew

that they were naked" (Gen. 3:7). As we commonly do when we sin, they tried to deceive God. They made coverings for their nakedness out of fig leaves, and when they heard the voice of God they tried to hide. When God called out, "Where are you?" Adam finally appeared and made a fourfold confession (Gen. 3:9):

(a) "I heard Your voice."

(b) "I was afraid." Adam and Eve had never known fear before. Now that they had sinned, they experienced guilt and fear.

(c) "I was naked." Before they sinned, they had been clothed in innocence, free from guilt and the fear of judgment; but now as sinners they feared their Creator, who made them, loved them, and provided for them.

(d) "I hid myself." God knew where they were, but Adam thought that they were well concealed. He soon learned that you cannot hide from our omnipotent, omniscient, omnipresent God!

At the first mention of fear, God was gracious and merciful. He provided a covering of animal skins for Adam and Eve before He removed them from the Garden of Eden (Gen. 3:21). He gave them the promise of a Redeemer, who would come and shed His blood and cover their sins.

The last mention of fear in the Bible is in Revelation 21:8. There we come to the end of all the dispensations of mankind, from Adam to the new heaven and the new earth. And the Lords says, "But the cowardly, unbelieving, abominable, murderers, sexually immoral, sorcerers, idolaters, and all liars shall have their part in the lake which burns with fire and brimstone, which is the second death" (Rev. 21:8.)

(4) *Fear of serving God in fleshly wisdom.* The apostle Paul journeyed to Corinth and preached the gospel of the Lord Jesus Christ. Later he wrote back to the church at Corinth, "I was with you in weakness, in fear, and in much trembling." Paul was saying, in effect, "When I preached the gospel to you in Corinth, I feared lest I should do it in fleshly wisdom"; therefore, "my speech and my preaching were not with persuasive words of human wisdom, but in demonstration of the Spirit and of power" (1 Cor. 2:1-5). Fear of serving God in the energy of the flesh is a good fear. We should strive to "do all in the name of the Lord Jesus, giving thanks to God the Father through Him" (Col. 3:17).

(5) *Fear of the end times.* At the end of the dispensation of the church age, and at the beginning of the Great Tribulation, "they will fall by the edge of the sword, and be led away captive into all nations. And Jerusalem will be trampled by Gentiles until the times of the Gentiles are fulfilled" (Luke 21:24). The "times of the Gentiles" will end with the Tribulation.

(6) *Fear of death.* The Lord Jesus Christ came to earth to die on Calvary, where He conquered death. To the believer, there need be no fear of death. Death has been conquered; death has been defeated. Through death Jesus destroyed "him who had the power of death, that is, the devil." He defeated Satan and death, delivering "those who through fear of death were all their lifetime subject to bondage" (Heb. 2:14, 15). It is sad to see many who profess to believe in the Lord Jesus Christ, yet live in the dread of physical death. When Jesus returns to this earth, He will raise the bodies of all the saints who have experienced physical death. The Word of God tells us, "There shall be no more death" (Rev. 21:4). This will be the end of death and fear for all eternity.

Fear Not: God Is Your Protector (Genesis 15:1)—"After these things the word of the LORD came to Abram in a vision" (v. 1). This was the fifth time the Lord manifested Himself to Abram—later named Abraham (Gen. 17:5).

(1) The first manifestation was in Ur of the Chaldeans (Gen. 11:31, cf. Acts 7:1-4).

(2) The second manifestation was in Haran where the Lord reaffirmed His call and promise to Abram (Gen. 12:1-4).

(3) The third manifestation was in Canaan, the promised land (Gen. 12:7).

(4) The fourth manifestation was in Canaan, after Lot was separated from him (Gen. 13:14, 15).

(5) The fifth manifestation was in Hebron. After Lot was separated from Abram, the latter moved his herd and all his servants away to Hebron, which became his pilgrim. Because this great man of faith was now experiencing fear, the Lord appeared to Abram, saying, "Do not be afraid, Abram. I am your shield, your exceedingly great reward" (v. 1). Why was Abram afraid? What did he fear? Abram was the friend of God. He talked with God person-to-person, as the Lord manifested Himself to him, but he still was afraid. He is the only man in the Bible called God's friend, yet he was afraid.

We must understand Abram's fear in the context of that we know about him. Chedorlaomer was king of Elam, a country east of Babylon. He was allied with three other ruthless kings. Five other kings of the Jordan valley, including the kings of Sodom and Gomorrah, had paid tribute to Chedorlaomer for twelve years. In the thirteenth year they rebelled (Gen. 14:1-4). In the fourteenth year these four kings, with their armies, invaded the Jordan valley, sacked Sodom and Gomorrah, defeated their armies, took all their wealth, and captured women and men, including Abram's nephew Lot. When the news reached Abram, he armed his 318 servants and pursued the numerically superior army into Dan. By night he divided his 318 men, then attacked the army while they were sleeping and defeated them. The Word of God tells us that when he returned from the slaughter, he brought back the captives and all the wealth they had taken.

Now we can answer the question, "What did Abram fear?" Most likely he feared reprisal. He had defeated an army; he had humiliated them with 318 servants—perhaps men without experience in battle. He feared that these four vanquished kings would return and invade Hebron. He was afraid, and rightly so, from the human standpoint. But God appeared to him and said, "Do not be afraid, Abram. I am your shield." In effect, God was saying, "I am your protector. Abram, you don't have to fear those barbarians, those wicked, ruthless kings. I am God Almighty; I will shield you; I will keep My promises and make you a great nation; I will give this land to your descendants. Abram, don't fear!"

Then the Lord said, "[I am] your exceedingly great reward." Abram, returning from the battle, was approached by the king of Sodom, who came out and told Abram to keep all the wealth that he had recovered—leaving him only with the people he had rescued. Abram replied that he would not take even a shoelace "lest you should say, 'I have made Abram rich'" (Gen. 14:23). Abram would not give anyone the opportunity to take credit for the way in which God had blessed him. God had blessed Abram and made him one of the richest men of all times. Abram honored God and sought only His glory. For Abram's faithfulness God rewarded him with heaven's highest honor: "I am your shield, your exceedingly great reward."

Fear Not: God Is Your Power (2 Kings 6:16)—"Do not fear, for those who are with us are more than those who are with them" (v. 16). Elisha was a prophet with great faith. By that faith he knew that the Lord's army was encamped around Dothan, not to save the city but to deliver Elisha from the hands of Ben-Hadad, king of Syria. The king had sent his army to capture Elisha because the Lord had revealed to the prophet all of Ben-Hadad's military plans. Elisha, in turn, revealed those plans to Ben-Hadad's enemy, Jehoram, king of Israel, thus guaranteeing Ben-Hadad's defeat. So Ben-Hadad sent spies to locate Elisha. When Elisha was found, the king sent horses, chariots, and a great army, just to capture one unarmed prophet! But they were not enough (v.14). They reached Dothan in darkness and surrounded the city. When Elisha's servant went about his morning duties, he saw the Syrian army and rushed in to Elisha, overcome by fear and crying, "Alas, my master! What shall we do?" (v. 15).

(1) Elisha taught the young man faith and the fear of the Lord. Elisha prayed that the Lord would open the young man's eyes so that he might see the unseen (v. 17; cf. 2 Cor. 4:18). Only by faith can we see the invisible host of heaven and "not fear." The Lord opened the young man's spiritual eyes, and he saw God's army ready to protect His servant.

(2) Every servant of God has the edge over the enemies of righteousness. The psalmist said, "The LORD is on my side; I will not fear. What can man do to me?" (Ps. 118:6). The believer has these armaments in his fight against fear:

   (a) *God's Word.* "For He Himself has said, 'I will never leave you nor forsake you.' So we may boldly say: The LORD is my helper; I will not fear. What can man do to me?" (Heb. 13:5, 6; cf. Deut. 31:12, 13).

   (b) *God's power.* "This poor man cried out, and the LORD heard him, and saved him out of all his troubles. The angel of the LORD encamps all around those who fear Him, and delivers them" (Ps. 34:6, 7).

   (c) *God's Holy Spirit.* "My Spirit remains among you; do not fear" (Hag. 2:5). "I will pray the Father, and He will give you another Helper [the Holy Spirit], that He may abide with you forever" (John 14:16).

   (d) *God's protection.* Isaiah said, "Be strong, do not fear! Behold, your God will come with vengeance, with the recompense of God; He will come and save you" (Is. 35:4). Isaiah 35 is a promise and a prophecy. "Be strong, do not fear! Behold, your God will come with vengeance." The promise is that the Messiah will come to establish God's kingdom on earth

(Rev. 19:11-16). The prophecy is that He will come with vengeance—at Armageddon (Rev. 19:17-21).

(3) While we wait for His second coming we are to "be strong in the Lord and in the power of His might." How? "Put on the whole armor of God, that you may be able to stand against the wiles of the devil" (Eph. 6:10, 11). Without God's armor, we fight a losing battle. God's armor consists of the following:

(a) *The belt of truth.* "Having girded your waist with truth" (Eph. 6:14). This belt of truth is embodied in Christ. Jesus said, "And you shall know the truth, and the truth shall make you free" (John 8:31, 32). Again He said, "I am . . . the truth" (John 14:6). Every believer must bear witness to the truth (John 5:33).

(b) *The breastplate of righteousness.* "Having put on the breastplate of righteousness" (Eph. 6:14). This breastplate is the righteousness of the Lord Jesus Christ (Rom. 10:1-4). It must be reflected in our daily lives.

(c) *The gospel shoes.* "Having shod your feet with the preparation of the gospel [good news] of peace" (Eph. 6:15). Christ is our peace, and without His gospel the sinner can never be at peace with God (Rom. 5:1). It is our duty to go with the gospel—to tell those who do not know it.

(d) *The shield of faith.* "Above all, taking the shield of faith" (Eph 6:16). Christ is our shield of faith. God said to Abram, "Do not be afraid, Abram. I am your shield" (Gen. 15:1). "The just shall live by faith" (Heb. 10:38). The shield of faith will quench all the fiery darts of the satanic kingdom.

(e) *The helmet of salvation.* "Take the helmet of salvation" (Eph. 6:17). Christ is our deliverance (Luke 4:16-18).

(f) *The sword of the Spirit.* "The sword of the Spirit [Holy Spirit], which is the word of God" (Eph. 6:17). Christ also is the sword, the living Word (John 1:1, 14). Let us exalt this Word in all that we do or say, and let us use it, our only *offensive* weapon.

(g) *Prayer.* "Praying always with all prayer and supplication in the Spirit" (Eph. 6:18). The armor is God's, and as good soldiers

of the cross we need to keep it polished with prayer. It is our
"secret defense!"

"Be strong, do not fear! Behold, your God will come with vengeance" (Is.
35:4). Until then, put on the whole armor of God and do not fear, because
"we are more than conquerors through Him who loved us" (Rom. 8:37).

From Bethlehem to Bikini

TEXT: LUKE 2:1-20

SOME of you will want to know why we bring Bikini into a discussion on Christmas season when what we want to do is to center our attention on Bethlehem.

The answer to that one is easy enough. I am not bringing Bikini into the picture. It's already in! It cannot be left out of consideration at this or any other season of the year because it has invaded and stands as a central threat in every area of thought and life known to man. To ignore or neglect this fact is more than a bit of wishful thinking conjured up by the undoubted magic of the Christmas season; it is an intellectual and spiritual betrayal of Christ.

Hard words, you say. Yes, but not half hard enough. For mere words cannot do justice to the hard fateful choice before every responsible man and nation today. And, better than anything else, Bethlehem and Bikini are symbols of the alternatives between which we must choose, if we have not already chosen. The spiritual pilgrimage of our generation is going to be to one or the other; it cannot be to both.

Certain characteristics of Bethlehem and Bikini invite comparison. Both are small places, geographically. Bethlehem—one of the smallest cities in ancient Palestine when it stepped into the spotlight of history; Bikini—one of the smallest coral atolls in the southern Pacific, so small that only the professional geographer knew where it was before it became known to everyone. Yet something occurred in both places to propel them into the center of world interest.

In each case this tremendous "something" was a dealing in the elemental stuff of the universe. Each event unlocked a new dimension of meaning for life and history. Bethlehem's discovery lay in the spiritual basis of life, in the realm of Divine will and purpose. Bikini's discovery lay in the material and physical basis of the universe—in the area of atomic structure, particularly unstable atomic structure. Bethlehem's revelation centers in a baby; Bikini's in a bomb. Bethlehem is the symbol of "Good tidings of great joy which shall be to all people. For unto you is born this day in the city of David a Saviour, which is Christ the Lord." Bikini is the symbol of the grim news of the stark menace with now confronts all people, for it shows man perfecting the power which actually can obliterate himself and his civilization.

Bethlehem is the symbol of God's mightiest effort to save the world. Bethlehem, celebrating the mystery of Divine love, exalts love as the central virtue in life. Bikini, celebrating the mastery of power, exalts power as the decisive factor in life. Bethlehem is the symbol of "Glory to God in the highest and on earth peace, goodwill toward men." Bikini is the symbol of the fact that man's life is rapidly becoming one long journey through fear, during which he will be separated from and finally lost to all he loves and seeks to save for himself and his children.

Bethlehem is the symbol of the beginning of a new era in human life and history. Bikini is the symbol of the beginning of the end of civilization.

That accounts for the fact that only a few people seemed to be aware of the meaning of the miracle of Bethlehem as it occurred, while the whole world watched Bikini with bated breath. A few shepherds, stirred by the angel's song, hurried to the manger in Bethlehem. But everyone else was quite unmoved by what seemed to be the ordinary fact that a girl from Galilee had given birth to a son. That was not even "news," let alone good news, when it occurred.

But Bikini was quite different. For weeks and months it was anticipated by press and radio. Its awesome importance was hammered home to every thinking person. When it occurred, the news was flashed everywhere, and people were listening. This is how one man recalls the day: I happened to be on a motor trip through Florida when the first bomb was dropped. I sought out a radio in a curio shop, hoping to hear the broadcast of the event. Business was at a standstill in the shop. Everyone gravitated toward the radio and we were chilled into silence by the tick, tick, tick of the metronome as the fateful moment approached. No fiction writer—not even Edgar Allan Poe—ever achieved such suspense as that! And when it was over one man, struggling to be optimistic, said to me: "Maybe it wasn't so bad after all."

Remembering the official report of what had happened at Hiroshima, I was not able to match his optimism, and replied: "It was probably a lot worse than we are able to imagine. We will never know how bad it really is until it hits us; then it will be too late to do anything about it."

He looked at me for a moment and then said: "Pessimistic, huh?"

Just so he wouldn't be in doubt on that point I said: "I wouldn't give a plugged nickel for our chances of using that bomb wisely."

The girl behind the counter added her bit: "After the first one hits us we won't care how many others come!"

If Bethlehem is the symbol of love, if Christina Rossetti is right when she sings:

> Love came down at Christmas,
> Love all lovely, love divine;
> Love was born at Christmas,
> Star and angel gave the sign,

then in contrast, Bikini is the symbol of fear and despair: *fear* because we know now that we can make the inhabited places of the earth a sea of fire; *despair* because we are afraid that that is just what we are going to do.

This series of contrasts between Bethlehem and Bikini must make it clear that they symbolize radically different ways of thought and standards of value. They amount actually, to two tragically different kinds of religion: a religion of the immeasurable love of God and a religion of the incalculable fear of each other.

No reconciliation between faiths like these is possible. It's one or the other. We can no more worship at the manger of Bethlehem and the lagoon of Bikini than we can serve God and mammon—and we have it on good authority that that just cannot be done.

Yet many of us are trying to do it. We nod our heads approvingly over Oliver Cromwell's admonition to his embattled Puritan soldiers: "Trust God and keep your powder dry." And, like Cromwell, we are considerably more careful about keeping the powder dry than we are about cultivating a strong trust in God. That is why we feel double-business bound at this time of the year. For Christmas centers in Bethlehem; in the incomprehensible love of God; in the mystery of the incarnation; in the tremendous fact of Immanuel—God with us; in love as the fundamental law of life; in the Kingdom of God as the fitting goal for the good life. Whoever takes these amazing facts at anything like face value knows that they both open the door and lay him under the unlimited obligation to become "a new creation in Christ." They are the New Testament; they are the Gospel; they are the beating heart of the Christian faith.

But as we prepare like the Magi of old to make a pilgrimage to Bethlehem and kneel in humble adoration at the side of Christ, Bikini taps us on the shoulder and presents us with another set of fundamental facts and asks that we order our thought and life according to them.

How utterly different they are! *Power*—pride in a power; mistrust of all others who may have or get this power; a determination to be ready to use it immediately and decisively, *i.e.*, ruthlessly, if and when the occasion should arise; a reluctant will to share the secret of the meaning of this power with any one, even our friends. *Fear*—the kind of nervous, excitable fear that chips away at stable relationships of trust and cooperation until they weaken and break; the kind of brooding, paralyzing feat that keeps us from new adventures in trust and cooperation, and emasculated existing organs for inter-communication. This is the way of life to which Bikini calls. To follow it is to turn our back on Bethlehem—not as a place but as the symbol of the hope of the world.

It is not necessary to outline the claims of Bikini or to list and consider the arguments which document them. We can trust the daily press and radio to do that. Most of the leaders in public thought and life are on pilgrimage to Bikini today, both in word and deed. So we can count on the fact that the case of Bikini both is and will continue to be carefully presented

But we may be sure that if Christian churches do not present the claims of Bethlehem, they will not be presented. It is desperately necessary and altogether appropriate for us therefore to outline the claims of Bethlehem and to keep them before ourselves and to present them to the world as the only true and realistic appraisal of the conditions of immediate survival and the hope for ultimate triumph.

The claims of Bethlehem grow out of what the Christian faith believes occurred there. It was more than the birth of a baby; it was the revelation in history of the love of God for man. It was the clearest and the most persuasive presentation of that love that God had or has ever made.

The wonder of it all has amazed men from that day to this. The writings of Matthew and Luke combine to give us a vivid picture of how intimations of the importance of the event ran everywhere even then. From humble shepherds who hurried to worship Him to haughty Herod who sent soldiers to slay Him; from unlettered men to learned men who shared the common assurance that in Him God was working a mighty work of fulfillment and redemption. For the human heart of Israel had longed for the day when God would fulfill their high hopes of seeing His Anointed come to usher in the Kingdom of God. And the human heart of all men longed for the moment and the One in whose life Heaven and earth would be united, man and God be reconciled. Hopes and longings like these echo through the great writings of Jew and gentile alike in the ancient world, giving them an air of expectancy and anticipation that is almost pathetic because it seemed to be so far from fulfillment. Then came Bethlehem with both fulfillment and redemption!

Is it any wonder that Gospel writers were sure the very angels in Heaven heralded the event? And that even the stars in the sky shone with a peculiar radiance in celebration of His coming?

Later Christian writers may have used less lyrical words in describing the meaning of Bethlehem, but they did not alter the meaning. The writer of the Gospel of John says that in Christ the love of God as an active, sacrificial concern for all men was revealed: "For God so loved the world that He gave His only Son that whoever believes in Him should not perish but have eternal life."

Paul, writing to the Corinthians about the meaning of the Christian faith, says: " . . . If anyone is in Christ, he is a new creation; the old has passed away, behold the new has come. All this is from God, who through Christ reconciled us to Himself and gave us the ministry of reconciliation; that is, God was in Christ reconciling the world unto Himself, not counting their trespasses against them, and entrusting to us the message of reconciliation."

Mr. T. S. Eliot, a modern poet, finds in the event of Christ's birth the only answer to the riddle of life and history:

> A moment not out of time, but in time, in what we call history;
> Transecting, bisecting the world of time, a moment in time but
> Not like a moment of time.
> A moment in time but time was made through that moment:
> For without the meaning there is no time, and that moment
> Of time gave the meaning.

It is the firm and united conviction of the Christian faith that this is what actually happened in Bethlehem on that first Christmas Eve. For ancient and modern seers alike, Bethlehem is God's supreme effort to awaken man from his nightmare of selfishness, greed, passion, and hatred to his true destiny as a child of God. Not by whirlwind and fire but by His Son was the effort made. Paul grasps and sets forth this grand strategy of redemption in one vivid sentence. "In the fullness of time God sent forth His Son . . ."

And our religious forefathers knew, as every man must know, that this approach of God in love requires and deserves an active response from man. Just as a newly freed slave is both dazed and delighted in his freedom, so Paul and his comrades kept breaking into shouts of joy as they sought the proper response to God's effort. One of the great students of the life of Paul, casting about for an adequate explanation of his sudden conversion, settled on this: "It was this coming of God to meet him that utterly conquered him." And it conquered others besides Paul. The writer of First John could say with searching simplicity: "Brethren, if God so loved us, we ought also to love one another."

These men knew, as we must know, that the intention of God in Christ is not a theatrical spectacle to be gaped at; it is an invitation to be accepted or rejected by every man. An invitation to a new relationship with God which carries as an inseparable corollary the responsibility of seeking a new relationship with men. Not without good cause were the early Christians identified as "followers of the way"—for the Christian faith is not so much a private attitude as it is a public way of life. I could wish that in these latter days we spoke less about accepting Christ and more about following Him. He wanted and wants followers; He was and is in search of disciples; the final note in His appeal was not and is not "sit and think" but "go and do."

Go and do what? Live as citizens of the Kingdom of God! Conduct ourselves and our affairs as befit those who find in the Sermon on the Mount the guiding ideals for living, who find in Jesus Christ our clearest revelation of God's will for man. Cultivate a forgiving spirit toward any injury and indignity. Be prepared to help any and all needy people as best you know how and can. Center your life in the reality of the Kingdom of God, put it first in your thinking and planning for the present and future. Accept as your supreme vocation the call to be "co-workers together with God" in the further realization of that Kingdom of Love in the affairs of man.

We shall not need to be warned that Christians have never found it easy to make love the central motive and force for living. They have always subordinated it to or at best driven it in double harness with other values like justice, security, and freedom. But that is spiritual betrayal of the Kingdom of God. To do that is to turn from Bethlehem to Bikini. For in the Kingdom inaugurated in Bethlehem *love is central.*

The late William Temple put it exactly right when he said: "The Kingdom of God is the sovereignty of Love, and the subordination of power to Love is the principle of that Kingdom." There is a Christ-sized job for the Christian fellowship today: the subordination of power to love; the subordination of selfish concern to mutual welfare; the subordination of the luxuries of the few to the necessities of the many; the subordination of political, social, and economic conventions to the welfare of every hungry, dispossessed, disenfranchised child of God.

The greatest living historian, Dr. Arnold Toynbee, said this: "Christianity places our conduct in this life on earth in its gigantic setting of infinity and eternity, and by opening our eyes to this vast spiritual vision it calls out our deepest spiritual energies." One of our most thoughtful social scientists, Dr. Pitirm Sorokin, said this: "There must be a change of the whole mentality and attitudes of our day in the direction of the norms prescribed in the Sermon on the Mount.

Long before Bikini dramatized our devotion to power as the great god of life, men like these sensed the deep and desperate spiritual malady of our culture. They knew what Christian prophets have always known—that Bethlehem is the only true symbol of hope and life for mankind. To turn the face of civilization from Bikini to Bethlehem is the great spiritual task of our generation, and one of the greatest spiritual tasks to confront any generation.

You wish we had a smaller or an easier job! And so do I! But no amount of wishing, much less whimpering, can lift the spiritual burden which rests upon us and our generation.

Strangely enough, there is one point of real agreement between Bethlehem and Bikini. When Mr. William L. Lawrence, science editor for "The New York Times," saw the bombs at Bikini he reached the conclusion that there was no defense against them and that "war must go." Mr. Bernard Baruch, elder statesman through two world wars, in the introduction to the report of the Atomic Control Commission said that the abolition of war represents the only real measure of safety against the bomb. Generals Eisenhower and MacArthur agreed. Senator Carl Hatch, chairman of the President's Evaluation Committee, underscores this fact: *war must go*. Bethlehem is in complete agreement with this position. From that day to this, men have believed in abolition of war and the dawn of a reign of peace and goodwill among men. So far no one has ever thought this task would be easy to fulfill.

The spiritual tragedy of western civilization can be put in a single sentence: It has not been able either to forget or to follow the vision of Bethlehem. With Bethlehem in its heart, its prayer, its art, its faith, it has nonetheless blundered along until it has found its way to Bikini. Needing above all else to kneel humbly at the manger in Bethlehem, finding thereby the true inspiration for human life and history, it has found itself watching a tiny lagoon in a faraway portion of the earth, conscious of the fact that there was being enacted the drama of its own destruction.

When Phillips Brooks, the great American preacher, was visiting the Holy Land he went on Christmas Eve to a height overlooking Bethlehem. It was there and then he wrote the poem:

> O little town of Bethlehem
> How still we see thee lie!
> Above thy deep and dreamless sleep
> The silent stars go by;
> Yet in thy dark street shineth
> The everlasting Light;
> The hopes and fears of all the years
> Are met in thee tonight

What he saw we see; what he felt to be true we know to be true. "The hopes and fears of all the years are met in thee tonight."

We have reason to be fearful, for we are part of a night pilgrimage from Bethlehem to Bikini. It will take a tremendous faith in the reality of God and the leadership of Jesus Christ to turn the face of our generation from Bikini to Bethlehem. But the star of hope continues to shine—over Bethlehem and nowhere else.

Gambling—Higher Style

TEXT: *And they crucified him, and parted his garments, casting lots.—*
MATTHEW 27:35

THE DRUGSTORE clerk said: "Mister, who won the third race?" We knew he meant a horse race and not the human race, but there our information ended. But his face was flushed: the question seemed almost a life and death concern to him. Times do not greatly change. The soldiers gambled for Christ's garments. Their action meant that He was as good as dead—and He saw them. It would be hard to imagine worse cruelty. He had five articles of clothing: a tunic, an outer robe, a turban, a girdle, and sandals—His whole worldly wealth. Who wore them afterwards?

The soldiers gambled. The clothes of a condemned man were then the perquisite of his executioners, and they cast dice for the booty. Plainly they were past feeling, or they would have waited until He had died. But is gambling always wrong? Surely there is a harmless kind? Perhaps. But the harmless kind, if it exists, is still like a lion-cub in the house: the pet, if uncurbed, becomes a ravenous beast.

Then what *is* wrong with it? If a man wins, he has no right to his gain, for a man is entitled only to earnings or free gifts. A certain student took a flyer on the market on the strength of inside information, and was bragging about his profits. An old Scotch professor asked quietly: "Did you earn it? Was it given?" Then he added yet more quietly: "Somebody lost it." If on the other hand a man loses he is guilty of waste, and knows it. So, winning or losing, he is in a bad light. Moreover the gambling soon becomes an absorbing passion, a fixed idea: the gambler is plainly warped. Moreover he warps other lives to the point of cruelty. You know the sorry story: defalcations at the bank, hunger in the home, and the disease still burning and burning. The money with which we gamble is not ours: the earth is God's, and we are only His trustees. What if all gambling is gambling for the garments of God?

So much for that: we are concerned with vaster issues. Caiaphas and Pilate gambled. Perhaps that was inescapable in some form, for life is a venture for every man. Edmund Burke declared that "gaming is a principle inherent in human nature." It is fairly certain that racetrack betting will never be overcome by repressive measures or condemnation. Perhaps the victory will come through "sublimation"—if you like that modern jargon: through transforming a poor kind of gambling into a higher style. You cannot walk down the street without taking risks. Some witty person has said that in New York traffic there are two kinds of pedestrians—the quick and the dead. You cannot conduct a business without venture, for there is no infallible way of knowing if a policy or an investment will succeed. The farmer is a gambler, for how can he tell if the weather will destroy his crops or bring them to harvest? All discovery is by risk. Reasoned planning may carry us so far, but beyond that point we must venture. Wise people do not rebel against that rule; for if life had no uncertainties it could have no zest, and perhaps we could have no growth.

This necessity to venture hold in the high matters of the soul. Shall we live for the noisy world or for the "still small voice" of conscience? For the moment or for eternity? Reason offers some guidance. It is at least as reasonable to suppose that a universe that has brought forth personal life is governed by a Personal God, as to believe that all creation is a galvanized spasm. It is as intelligent to judge life by its best, namely, the spirit of Jesus, as to judge it by its worst, namely, a devilishness or deadness that gambles at the foot of the Cross. But reason cannot prove, either by logic or scientific demonstration, that conscience is a better treasure than cash. If it could, men might be good for common-sense advantage—in which instance real goodness would vanish. No, we must take the risk, on the body against the soul, or on the soul against the body.

So Caiaphas and Pilate gambled. On what? On the faith (if faith it can be called) that the sword rules, that death is the end of a man, and that selfishness brings joy to the selfish. They bet on the proposition that God is not watching, or that He does not care. They could not prove their faith, but they took the chance. They would have told you: "It is a sure thing, like money in the bank." Frank Bets (appropriate name) has a poem about it, addressed to Judas Iscariot:

You sold Him and you thought Him slain,
And the old proud game begins again,
And Caesar plays with might and main.
But a hidden Player has the Black,
And the craft is foiled, and the White attack
Move by move is beaten back,
Iscariot.
Knight nor Bishop can resist
The pawns of this Antagonist
Whose countenance is dark with mist.
The game goes on and will not wait,
Caesar is gripped in a deadly strait—
What if the pawns should give checkmate,
Iscariot?

Caiaphas and Pilate gambled. It seemed that they could not miss. Was there a Hidden Player on the other side of the board?

Let us say reverently that there was another gambler at Calvary: Jesus gambled. While the soldiers were casting lots for His garments, He ventured His soul on God for the love of mankind. "I, if I be lifted up from the earth, will draw all men unto me."

"Lifted up" means crucified in shame. What a hazard! Someone may say: "But Jesus knew that God was on His side." He knew by faith. He did not know by visible fact or proven logic. His soul said "Yes," but His pain-racked body still said "No."

Golgotha is a word that means The Place of a Skull. Perhaps the name was given because the hilltop was littered with skulls, perhaps because it was shaped like a skull. In either event it declared silently that a skull is the last word about man's life. But Jesus made His venture, while other men cast lots for His garments. Jesus cried out to God: "Father, forgive them. Father, into Thy hands I commit my spirit."

His plea is that you and I should live in that self-same venture. He condemned the one-talent man, not because he had only one talent, but because he buried it in the earth instead of risking it in the traffic of the world. He bade His disciples: "Launch out into the deep!"—and had in mind more than their craft as fishermen. He constantly insisted, in crucial and cardinal teaching, that only "he that loseth his life shall find it."

Lose to win: there is the overturning of our human wisdom. Let a man lose his life in lowliness while others clamor for name and fame; let him lose his life in succoring human need while others seek the main chance; let him die like a seed dies in the dark earth. Thus Jesus ventured in the tremendous risk of the Cross.

When the Japanese first marched into China at the onset of the last world war, Heywood Broun wrote a column entitled "It Shall Come Back." Thus he prophesied that the ravaged land would be returned to the Chinese. At the moment the prediction seemed folly. China had fallen among thieves, and other nations were like the priest and the Levite in the story: they "passed by on the other side." There was no Good Samaritan. Our nation sold scrap iron to the aggressor. But it came back, and would have come back if no war has been fought. The Chinese have quietly absorbed the conqueror long before our time. "The mills of God grind slowly, but they grind exceeding small."

Could anyone have guessed on the first Good Friday that Jesus would "Come Back?" His death was more than death: it was an oblivion of shame. But Caiaphas and Pilate are now remembered, in pity or execration, only because of their victim. Jesus is not forgotten. The tragedy now is the revealing of the sorrow of God for the cleansing of our soul, and beyond the tragedy Jesus returned—because He hazarded His soul in death.

You and I must gamble—higher style. Donald Hankey has written: "Religion is betting your life there is a God." Perhaps he should have said: "High religion is betting your life there is a Christ like God."

It is not a blind bet. Reason gives as much support, and perhaps more, to faith as to unfaith. But God is not a theorem, and therefore cannot be proved. If he is a Person He can be known only in the venture of prayer and deed. How else? The Epistle to the Philippians has a fine sentence about a man called Epaphroditus who at risk aided Paul, when Paul was in prison for his Christian faith. Paul enjoins the Philippian church about the man: "Receive him therefore in the Lord with all gladness, . . . because for the work of Christ he was nigh unto death, staking his life"! Our version says: "not regarding his life." It means "having no regard for his life": the Greek word is one used of gamblers—"staking his life."

When all arguments are made and ended, if they are ever ended, you and I must stake our life. How are you betting? Like the soldiers? Have a care! That kind of gambling is at best the turning of life into a casual pastime, and at worst a destroying fever. Then how are you betting? Like Pilate?

It is an old game, and our world is still busy at it; Pilate's game,
Whose game was empires, and whose stakes were thrones
Whose table earth—whose dice were human bones.

Do not bet that money or fame will bring you happiness, let alone blessedness. Do not bet time against eternity. Do not bet that God is not looking, or that there is no heaven or hell: the skeptic may be very surprised the first moment after death.

Then how will you bet? Like Christ? You cannot: there is only one Christ. But you can bet that His suffering, as it cleanses you, is God's pardon; and you can venture your soul on Him for all eternity. You cannot prove the faith. If you could prove it you would be compelled to believe it; and then it would become, not a faith at all, but only a drab compulsion. There is enough evidence for Christ to provoke your venture, but never so much that you are spared the hazard.

A doctor in a quiet northern town heard one winter that there was an epidemic in a lonely island out in the lake. His methods as a doctor were hardly according to modern hygiene. The strips of adhesive tape stuck on the varnished door had been there a long time, and the scissors with which he removed bandages were more like rusty garden shears. But he had a great heart.

He must reach that island. But how? No boat could go through the ice those forty or fifty miles. Perhaps an aeroplane could make the trip. But the airport was poor enough in summer, and almost impossible in winter. Yet he persuaded a pilot to make the journey, and they did not crash.

Was it worth the risk? Reason could have been enlisted on the side of safety; a very plausible argument could have been advanced that there were plenty of sick and needy people close at hand. But a man's soul gathered to that venture. There is a telling fact: a man's soul is fevered by low gambling, but fulfilled in any Christian venture. Surely the world and time and eternity also gather when the soul gathers. But you could not prove it—thank God. It is proved in the zest of the venture.

Why gamble in a cheap way when you can gamble in noble soul? Race-track stuff is childish and petty: the world waits for men who still will hazard their lives, day by day or in early death, for the sake of Christ.

You have seen the colored squares on the counter of a game of chance in a country fair. The world is your coin. Your soul is the coin. What shall a man give in exchange for his soul? Now, on what color—Pilate or Jesus? You say that you have tried it, and have found that the Christian life does not pay off? It depends what is meant by "pay off." You will have zest of soul that no other venture can give you: that is rather better than some money-itch. The log of Columbus read night after night: "And this day we sailed on" . . . "And this day we sailed on" . . . "And this day we sailed on." There was still no sight of land. But you live in America. The man who sails by faith in Christ will reach his celestial country. Or will he? You can prove it only in the venture. High religion is "betting your life" there's a Christlike God.

God's Will

(1) Although this world system is presently an organized kingdom of evil, ruled and motivated by the will of Satan, who is "the prince of the power of the air, the spirit who now works in the sons of disobedience" (Eph. 2:1-3), it must be remembered that Satan is not all-powerful. Only God has all authority over all power. God spoke to Isaiah saying, "I am God, and there is no other, I am God, and there is none like Me, declaring the end from the beginning . . . 'My counsel shall stand, and I will do all My pleasure'" (Is. 46:9, 10). It is God's pleasure to reveal His will (plan for your life) to all believers. Jesus told His disciples to get into a boat and go to the other side of Galilee. Being omniscient (all-knowing), He knew they would encounter a storm; being omnipotent (all-powerful), He knew that He would save them from the storm. This was His specific will for His disciples (Matt. 14:22, 23-33). In the will of God they were

(1) sent into a storm. The will of God is filled with storms. Every believer who walks in God's will encounters contrary winds. Paul faced opposing winds throughout his ministry (2 Cor. 11:24-33).
(2) In no danger, because Jesus was in prayer (Heb. 7:25).
(3) In darkness. No believer, who is in the will of God, will remain in darkness (John 12:46).
(4) Rowing with all their might against contrary winds. Nevertheless, they were making no progress (Mark 6:48).

When God puts it in your heart to do His will and you face contrary winds, remember that He will direct your path (Prov. 3:5, 6).

God's Will Is Sovereign
(Isaiah 46:9-11)

God's Will Is Immutable
(Malachi 3:6)
God's Will Is Good, Acceptable, and Perfect
(Romans 12:1, 2)
God's Will Can Be Known
(Hebrews 13:20, 21)
God's Will for Individuals
(Colossians 1:9, 10)

God's Will Is Sovereign (Isaiah 46:9-11)—"I am God, and there is none like Me, declaring the end from the beginning . . . My counsel shall stand, and I will do all My pleasure" (vv. 9, 10). These verses declare the fact that God's sovereign will is in control of all things in heaven and on earth and throughout His universe. No one can alter His purposes. He said, "I will do all My pleasure" (v. 10).

His sovereign will is established in the fulfilling of prophecy. He has declared the end, even from the beginning. He continued, "Indeed I have spoken it; I will also bring it to pass. I have purposed it; I will also do it" (v. 11). In context, God is saying that He has prophesied Israel's future, and will bring the prophecy to pass. What He has proposed, He will do. God's sovereign will determines the end of everything; His purpose cannot be circumvented (Dan. 4:35).

The part of God's sovereign will that is not revealed is often called His secret will. Though we cannot know all of God's sovereign will, by faith we can know that part revealed through the Scriptures (Deut. 29:29). Most of God's sovereign will is secret, and we cannot know His secret will until He is ready to reveal it (Acts 1:6, 7; Amos 9:11-15).

We can, however, know God's sovereign purpose in history for the Jew and the Gentile, for He has made it known to us in His Word. He said to Abraham, "I will make you a great nation . . . . and in you all the families [nations] of the earth shall be blessed" (Gen. 12:2, 3). His sovereign will for Israel is well established in the Old and New Testaments, beginning with His promise to make Abraham's seed a great nation (Israel), and to bless all the nations of the earth through his seed, which is Christ (Gal. 3:6-9). Ultimately, true Israel will be saved and enter the kingdom where Christ is King of kings (Rom. 11: 26-29; Matt. 25:31-46). We also know God's sovereign will for all who, by faith, will accept the Lord Jesus Christ as their personal Savior (John 3:16, 17). They are predestined for eternal life with God (John 14:1-6); but those who reject Christ as their personal Savior are predestined to the lake of fire (Rev. 20:15).

Calvary is a proof of God's sovereign will. About a thousand years before Christ died on the cross, David prophesied that the Messiah would be crucified (Ps. 22:14-18). About seven hundred years before Calvary, Isaiah prophesied the ignominious death of Jesus Christ, who suffered for our sins (Is. 52:13-53:12). God's will is sovereign.

God's Will Is Immutable (Malachi 3:6)—"For I am the LORD, I do not change" (v. 6). He does not change: "God is not a man, that He should lie, nor a son of man, that He should repent [change]. Has He said, and will He not do? Or has He spoken, and will He not make it good?" (Num. 23:19). God will keep His Word and perform His unchangeable will.

Note that according to God's unchangeable will, "all Israel will be saved . . . The Deliverer will come out of Zion, and He will turn away ungodliness from Jacob; for this is My covenant with them, when I take away their sins" (Rom. 11: 26, 27). This no more means that every Hebrew who ever lived will be saved than that every Gentile will be saved. But it does mean that all elect Jews (the remnant believers) will be saved. "The Redeemer will come to Zion" (Is. 59:20, 21), which refers to the second coming of Christ. Every good and perfect gift is a part of God's unchangeable will. "Of His own will He brought us forth by the word of truth" (James 1:17, 18). It is God's purpose that this "word of truth" (the gospel)—the death, burial, and resurrection of Jesus Christ—be preached to Israel, so that "all Israel will be saved." God's will was immutable (or unchangeable) yesterday, today, and forever (Heb. 13:8). God reveals His immutable will in His eternal Word.

God's will is immutable

(1) *in salvation.* We are saved by grace through faith, not through works (Eph. 2:8, 9; cf. Acts 4:12; Rom. 10:8-10).

(2) *In judgment.* "For the Father judges no one, but has committed all judgment to the Son" (John 5:22).

   (a) Christ will judge the believer's works at "the judgment seat of Christ" (2 Cor. 5:10), to take place at the rapture of the church (Rev. 22:12). Believers will be rewarded for their good works, but for their bad works they will suffer the loss of rewards, not the loss of salvation (1 Cor. 3:11-15). This is evidence that works alone cannot merit the salvation of God.

    (b)   Christ will judge all nations of the world at the beginning of His millennial reign (Matt. 25:31-46).

    (c)   Christ will judge the wicked at the end of His millennial reign (Rev. 20:11-15).

(3) *in morals*

    (a)   "You shall have no other gods before Me."

    (b)   "You shall not make for yourself a carved image."

    (c)   "You shall not take the name of the LORD your God in vain."

    (d)   "Honor your father and your mother."

    (e)   "You shall not murder."

    (f)   "You shall not commit adultery."

    (g)   "You shall not steal."

    (h)   "You shall not bear false witness against your neighbor."

    (i)   "You shall not covet" (Ex. 20:1-17).

To know God's immutable will, you must know His Word.

God's Will Is Good, Acceptable, and Perfect (Romans 12:1, 2)—Paul urges every believer to "prove [to yourself and others] what is that good and acceptable and perfect will of God" (v. 2). If you are a born-again believer and you do not know God's revealed will for your life, you are cheating yourself (living beneath your privilege) and grieving the Holy Spirit. God's revealed will is:

(1) *Good.* It is good in itself because it is God's will. It is good for you, and good to you. In the will of God, the believer can claim His promises, i.e., "For the LORD God is a sun and shield; the LORD will give grace and glory; no good thing will He withhold from those who walk uprightly" (Ps. 84:11). The key word in this promise is "give."

    (a)   "The LORD God" is the giver of every good and perfect gift (James 1:17).

    (b)   This Giver is a "sun and shield." He is the light of the world to guide you each step of the way as you walk in His will (John 8:12), and He is a shield to protect you (Ps. 3:2, 3).

    (c)   He gives "grace and glory." In the revealed will of God you know the grave of God that brings eternal riches. "For you know the grace of our Lord Jesus Christ, that though He was rich, yet for your sakes He became poor, that you through His poverty might become [eternally] rich" (2 Cor. 8:9). His glory is also a gift; can you think of a greater reward? He will share His grace and glory with those who do His good will (Rom. 8:17). Paul said, "hold fast what is good" (1 Thess. 5:21).

(2) *Acceptable.* God's revealed will is the only will that is acceptable to Him. Man's natural will is rebellious, or carnal (Rom. 8:6-8). Satan's will is totally evil (Is. 14:13, 14). Five times Satan said, "I will". Not once did he regard the will of God. The question is, to what degree does your will conform to God's will? You are either doing the will of Satan (which is evil), or the will of self (which is carnal), or the will of God (which is good, acceptable, and perfect). It is impossible to please God and walk in man's carnal way, or Satan's corrupt way (Eph. 2:1-3).

(3) *Perfect.* Because God is perfect, His will is perfect. His will is pleasing to His perfect nature, in the most infinitesimal detail. The will of God can be discovered and obeyed by every believer. Because He has revealed to us the mystery of His will in His Word (Eph. 1:9), God wants us to know and understand His revealed will, which is good, acceptable, and perfect (Eph. 5:17).

God's Will Can Be Known (Hebrews 13:20, 21)—In the old Adamic nature, we are not capable of knowing and doing the perfect will of God. To the unsaved, spiritual things are foolishness (1 Cor. 1:18). The unsaved may be religious, but they do not possess the spiritual capacity to discern spiritual things (1 Cor. 2:14). If you are a born-again, Spirit-filled believer who desires to know and do the perfect will of God, God will take control of your life and "make you complete in every good work to do His will" (v. 21).

God does have a plan for your life. He did not save you to let you go your way and make your own decisions, according to your carnal nature. God gives the believer a new nature to combat the ways of his old nature (2 Pet. 1:4). We have already seen that man's natural way is carnal, and that Satan's way is totally evil. But, God's way is perfect, and is the only way that pleases Him. It is impossible for a carnal, or rebellious, Christian to please God (Rom. 8:5-9). Therefore, it is imperative that you know the will of God for your life and do it.

The question is, how can I know the perfect will of God for my life?

(1) You must sincerely desire to do His will. This is an act of faith. "The just shall live by faith" (Heb. 10:38).

(2) You must search the Scriptures if you are going to know the will of God for your life. The apostle Paul tells us that the Bereans "were more fair-minded than those in Thessalonica, in that they received the word with all readiness, and searched the Scriptures daily to find out whether these things were so" (Acts 17:11). The Berean believers did two things—they heard and accepted the Word of God as it was preached, and they "searched the Scriptures daily to find out whether these things were so." The best way for believers to know the will of God for their lives is to search the Scriptures, which continually point to Christ (John 5:39). If you choose to "grow in the grace and knowledge of . . . Christ" (2 Pet. 3:18) through the study of His Word, God will equip you to know and live out His perfect plan for your life.

(3) If you sincerely desire to know God's will, you must recognize the ministry of the indwelling Holy Spirit.

    (a) He communicates with our spirit, always in harmony with the Scriptures, assuring us that we are the children of God (Rom. 8:16). When we are not sure of God's will in our daily decisions, we can trust the indwelling Holy Spirit to reveal His perfect will, because He always intercedes for the believer "according to the will of God" (Rom. 8:27).

    (b) Jesus promised the apostles that the Holy Spirit would guide them into all truth (John 16:13). Through the Scriptures the Holy Spirit also leads us into all the truth we need to know about God's will for our lives. The Holy Spirit will guide us day after day, as we walk according to the will of God revealed in the Scriptures (Eph. 1:9).

(4) You must read signs of God's providence. Jesus said to the Philadelphia church, "I know your works. See, I have set before you an open door, and no one can shut it" (Rev. 3:7, 8). When a church or an individual is living in God's perfect plan, God will open doors of service that no one can close (2 Cor. 2:12), or He will close doors that no one can open. You must be fully committed to Christ and His will before the Lord can show you His open doors. When you are seeking the will of God and there is before you an open door, wait upon the Lord (Is. 40:31). Pray as you wait—pray that the Lord will close the door to you

if you should not enter. Yes, God does use outward circumstances to reveal His will to us. If you have a desire to serve the Lord in a special ministry and the door is closed, don't try to force it open. Learn to wait on the Lord, and He will direct your path (Prov. 3:5, 6).

(5) Seek the counsel of godly leaders such as pastors, teachers, elders, deacons, and also parents and spiritually mature Christians (Prov. 11:14; 13:10).

God has a purpose—a perfect plan for every born-again child of God who desires to know and do His pleasure. If you sincerely desire God's will, He will cause everything to work together for your spiritual good (Rom. 8:28, 29).

God's Will for Individuals (Colossians 1:9-10 Are you filled with the knowledge of God's will for your life? Paul said he desired "that you may be filled with the knowledge of His will in all wisdom and spiritual understanding" (v. 9). This verse tells us God has a perfect plan for each believer, so that he or she can please Him and be fruitful in good works. Everyone can know God's will for his or her life in all spiritual wisdom and understanding. This spiritual wisdom does not come from within the natural (carnal) man (1 Cor. 2:14); it comes from the throne of God by the prayer of faith.

James tells us that there are two kinds of wisdom. The first is earthly wisdom, born of carnal man. It is a superficial sort of wisdom, a part of this world system that says, "If there is a God, we do not need Him." "This wisdom does not descend from above [from God], but is earthly [beastly], sensual [lust of the flesh], demonic [demon-controlled]. For where envy [jealousy] and self-seeking exist, confusion and every evil thing are there" (James 3:13-16). This earthly wisdom will never lead you into the perfect will of God.

The second kind is heavenly wisdom, and is a gift of God to all who meet the requirements in James 1:5-8. "But the wisdom that is from above is first pure, then peaceable, gentle, willing to yield, full of mercy and good fruits, without partiality and without hypocrisy" (James 3:17). This heavenly wisdom will reveal God's perfect will for your life when you seek it with your whole heart through prayer and His Word.

Wisdom to know the perfect will of God for your life is a gift of God; spiritual understanding comes from a knowledge of God's revealed will in the Scriptures (2 Tim. 2:15). "Therefore do not be unwise, but understand what the will of the Lord is" (Eph. 5:17). Yes, God wants you to know His specific plan for your life and understand that in it "all things work together for good to those who love God, to those who are the called according to His purpose" (Rom. 8:28).

We pray for spiritual wisdom to know the will of God. We pray for wisdom to read outward expressions of God's providence, to recognize open or closed doors, and always to be spiritually conscious of the indwelling Holy Spirit, who has promised to guide us into all truth. Remember that these outward and inward leadings never contradict the revealed will of God in His Word.

God has made known His perfect will to individuals in every Biblical age, and the evidence is overwhelming.

(1) In the age before the Flood, God revealed His plan to the following persons:

  (a) To Adam, when He placed him in the Garden of Eden (Gen. 2:15-17). When Adam and Eve sinned, God sent them out of the Garden and made known His will for them and their descendants, under the curse of sin (Gen. 3:1-2).
  (b) To Enoch, who walked with God for three hundred years (Gen. 5:18-24).
  (c) To Noah, who built the ark according to God's revealed instructions (Gen. 6:9-22).

(2) In the age of the patriarchs, from Abraham to Joshua, God revealed His plan to Abraham, whom He called and commissioned to walk in His will (Gen. 12:1-9). He failed in his first test and went down into Egypt (Gen. 12:10-20). He returned to Bethel, where he had built an altar, "And there Abram called on the name of the LORD" (Gen. 13:1-4). In Egypt he did not build an altar, nor did he call on the name of the Lord. He disobeyed the will of God when he chose his own course of action. No believer is capable of making the right decision merely on the basis of natural wisdom; Abraham was a wise man, but not that wise. When a believer has a decision to make, and he does not know the will of God, he can ask God for wisdom, "and it will be given to him. But let him ask in faith, with no doubting" (James 1:5-8).

(3) God raised up the judges, from Othniel to Samuel, to do His will. Some failed the Lord, others walked in His will.

(4) In the kingdom period (from King Saul to King Zedekiah) God, through the prophets, revealed His plan to the kings of Israel and Judah. Some kings rebelled and did evil, but others walked in His will and were blessed by God.

(5) In the church age Jesus said, "For I have come down from heaven, not to do My own will, but the will of Him who sent Me" (John 6:38). Jesus (the God-Man), whose will is as perfect as the Father's, united His will with the will of the Father. In this He is our great example. Therefore, we must seek to know and to do the will of God in everything (Col 3:16, 17). It would be difficult to mention all of the New Testament saints who walked in the will of God. Think of the millions of believers, since Jesus' day, who have walked in His will; add to that all the saints of the future who will know His plan for their lives and walk in it. Yes, God does have a perfect plan for your life; may you not rest until you know it, and learn how to walk in it.

Law and Grace

In his epistle to the Romans, Paul writes, "For as by one man's disobedience many were made righteous. Moreover the law entered, that the offence might abound. But where sin abounded, grace did much more abound: that as sin hath reigned unto death, even so might grace reign through righteousness unto eternal life by Jesus Christ our Lord" (Romans 5:19-21).

Moses was the representative of the law. He led the children of Israel through the wilderness and bought them to Jordan, but there he left them. He could take them up to the river, which is a type of death and judgment; but Joshua (which means Jesus—Savior) led them right through death and judgment—through the Jordan into the Promised Land. Here we have the difference between law and grace; between the law and the Gospel.

Take another illustration. John the Baptist was the last prophet of the old dispensation—the last prophet under the law. Before Christ made His appearance at the Jordan, the cry of John day by day was, "Repent: for the kingdom of God is at hand!" He thundered out the law. He took his hearers down to the Jordan and baptized them. He put them in the place of death; and that was as far as he could take them. But there was One coming after him who could take them into the Promised Land. As Joshua led the people through the Jordan into Canaan—so Christ went down into the Jordan of death, through death and judgment, on to resurrection ground.

All through the Scriptures, you will find that the law brings us to death. "Sin hath reigned unto death" (Romans 5:21). The story goes that a minister was once called upon to officiate at a funeral, in the place of a chaplain of one of Her Majesty's prisons, who was absent. He noticed that only one solitary man followed the body of the criminal to the grave. When the grave had been covered, this man told the minister that he was an officer of the law whose duty it was to watch the body of the culprit until it was buried out of sight; that was "the end" of the British law.

And that is what the law of God does to the sinner: it brings him right to death, and leaves him there. I pity deep down in my heart those who are trying to save themselves by the law. It never has, it never will, and it never can—save the soul. When people say they are going to try and do their best, and so save themselves by the law, I like to take them on their own ground. Have they ever done their very best? Granting that there *might* be a chance for them if they had, was there ever a time when they could not have done a little better? If a man wants to do his best, let him accept the grace of God; that is the best thing that any man or woman can possibly do.

But you will ask, What is the law give for? It may sound rather strange, but it is given that it may stop every man's mouth. "We know that what things so ever the law saith, it saith to them who are under the law: that every mouth may be stopped, and all the world may become guilty before God. Therefore by deeds of the law there shall no flesh be justified in his sight: for by the law is the knowledge of sin." The law shuts my mouth; grace opens it. The law locks up my heart; grace opens it—and then the fountain of love begins to flow out. When men get their eyes opened to see this glorious truth, they will cease their constant struggle. They will give themselves up for lost, and take salvation as a free gift.

Life never came through the law. As someone has observed, when the law was given, three thousand men lost life; but when grace and truth came at Pentecost, three thousand obtained life. Under the law, if a man became a drunkard, the magistrates would take him out and stone him to death. When the prodigal came home, grace met him and embraced him. Law says, Stone him!—Grace says, Embrace him! Law says, Smite him!—Grace says, Kiss him! Law went after him, and bound him; Grace said, Loose him and let him go! Law tells me how crooked I am; Grace comes and makes me straight.

A perfect God can only have a perfect standard. He that offends in one point is guilty of all; so "all have sinned, and come short of the glory of God."

Paul says to the Galatians: "Is the law then against the promises of God? God forbid: for if there had been a law given which could have given life, verily righteousness should have been by the law. But the scripture hath concluded all under sin, that the promise by faith of Jesus Christ might be given to them that believe. But before faith came, we were kept under the law, shut up unto the faith, which should afterwards be revealed. Wherefore the law was our schoolmaster to bring us unto Christ, that we might be justified by faith. But after the faith is come, we are no longer under a schoolmaster. For ye are all the children of God by faith in Christ Jesus" (3:21-26).

The Softening Power of Grace

So we see that the law cannot give life; all it can do is to bring us to Him who is the life. The law is said to be "a schoolmaster." Perhaps some of you do not know what a schoolmaster is. If you had been under the same schoolmaster as I was when a boy, you would have known. He had a good cane and it was frequently in use. In the little country district where I went to school, there were two parties; for the sake of illustration we may call the one the "law" party and the other the "grace" party. The law party said that boys could not possibly be controlled without the cane; and they kept a schoolmaster there who acted on their plan. The struggle went on, and at last, on one Election Day, the law party was put out, and the grace party ruled in their stead. I happened to be at the school that time; and I remember we said to each other that we were going to have a grand time that winter. There would be no more corporeal punishment, and we were going to be ruled by love.

I was one of the first to break the rules of the school. We had a lady teacher, and she asked me to stay behind. I thought the cane was coming out again; and I was going to protest against it. I was quite in a fighting mood. She took me alone. She sat down and began to talk to me kindly. I thought that was worse than the cane; I did not like it. I saw that she had not gotten any cane. She said: "I have made up my mind that if I cannot control the school by love, I will give it up. I will have no punishment; and if you love me, try and keep the rules of the school." I felt something right here in my throat. I was not one to shed many tears; but I could not keep them back. I said to her "You will have no more trouble with me"; and she did not. I learned more that winter than in the other three put together.

That was the difference between law and grace. Christ says, "If you love me, keep my commandments" (John 14:15). He takes us out from under the law, and puts us under grace. Grace will break the hardest heart. It was the love of God that prompted Him to send His only begotten Son into the world that He might save it. I suppose the thief had gone through his trail unsoftened. Probably the law had hardened his heart. But on the cross no doubt that touching prayer of the Savior, "Father, forgive them!" broke his heart, so that he cried, "Lord, remember me!" He was brought to ask for mercy.

It is told of Isaac T. Hopper, the Quaker, that he once encountered a profane colored man, named Cain, in Philadelphia, and took him before a magistrate, who fined him for blasphemy. Twenty years after, Hopper met Cain, whose appearance was much changed for the worse. This touched the friend's heart. He stepped up, spoke kindly, and shook hands with the forlorn being. "Dost thou remember me," said the Quaker, "how I had thee fined for swearing?"

"Yes, indeed, I do: I remember what I paid as well as if it was yesterday."

"Well, did it do thee any good?"

"No, never a bit; it made me mad to have my money taken from me."

Hopper invited Cain to reckon up the interest on the fine, and paid him principal and interest too. "I meant it for thy good, Cain; and I am sorry I did thee any harm."

Cain's countenance changed; the tears rolled down his cheeks. He took the money with many thanks, became a quiet man, and was not heard to swear again.

Peace, Grace and Glory

So there is a great deal of difference between law and grace. "Being justified by faith, we have peace with God through our Lord Jesus Christ: by whom also we have access by faith into this grace wherein we stand, and rejoice in hope of the glory of God" (Romans 5:1-2). There are three precious things here: peace for the past; grace for the present things here: peace for the past; grace for the present; and glory for the future. There is no *peace* until we see the finished work of Jesus Christ—until we can look back and see the cross of Christ between us and our sins. When we see that Jesus was "the end of the law for righteousness" (Romans 10:4); that He "taste [d] death for every man" (Hebrews 2:9); that He "suffered . . . the just for the unjust" (1 Peter 3:18)—then comes peace. Then there is "the *grace* wherein we now stand." There is plenty of grace for us as we need it—day by day, and hour by hour.

Then there is *glory* for the time to come. A great many people seem to forget that the best is before us. Dr. Bonar says that everything before the true believer is "glorious." This thought took hold of my soul; and I began to look the matter up, and see what I could find in Scripture that was glorious hereafter. I found that the kingdom we are going to inherit is glorious; our crown is to be a "crown of glory"; the city we are going to inhabit is the city of the glorified; the songs we are to sing are the songs of the glorified; we are to wear garments of "glory and beauty"; our society will be the society of the glorified; our rest is to be "glorious"; the country to which we are going is to be full of "the glory of God and of the Lamb." There are many who are always looking on the backward path, and mourning over the troubles through which they have passed. They keep lugging up the cares and anxieties they have been called on to bear, and are forever looking at them. Why should we go reeling and staggering under the burdens and cares of life when we have such prospects before us?

If there is nothing but glory beyond, our faces ought to shine brightly all the time. If a skeptic were to come up here and watch the countenances of the audience he would find many of you looking as though there was anything but glory before you. Many a time it seems to me as if I were at a funeral, people look so sad and downcast. They do not appear to know much of the joy of the Lord. Surely, if we were looking right on to the glory that awaits us, our faces would be continually lit up with the light of the upper world. We can preach by our countenances if we will.

The nearer we draw to that glory-land, where we shall be with Christ—the more peace, and joy, and rest we ought to have. If we will but come to the throne of grace, we shall have strength to bear all our troubles and trials. If you were to take all the afflictions that flesh is heir to and put them right on any one of us, God has grace enough to carry us right through without faltering.

Someone has compiled the following, which beautifully describes the contrast between law and grace:

THE LAW was given by Moses.
GRACE and truth came by Jesus Christ.
THE LAW says—This do, and thou shalt live.
GRACE says—Live, and then thou shalt do.
THE LAW says—Pay me what thou owest.
GRACE says—I frankly forgive thee all.
THE LAW says—The wages of sin is death
GRACE says—The gift of God is eternal life.
THE LAW says—The soul that sinneth, it shall die.
GRACE says—Whosoever believeth in Jesus, though he were dead, yet shall he live; and whosoever liveth and believeth in Him shall never die.
THE LAW pronounces—Condemnation and death.
GRACE proclaims—Justification and life.
THE LAW says—Make you a new heart and a new spirit.
GRACE says—A new heart will I give you, and a new spirit will I put within you.
THE LAW says—Cursed is every one that continueth not in all things which are written in the book of the law to do them.
GRACE says—Blessed is the man whose iniquities are forgiven, whose sin is covered; blessed is the man to whom the Lord will not impute iniquity.
THE LAW says—Thou shalt love the Lord thy God with all thy heart, and with all thy mind, and with all thy strength.
GRACE says—Herein is love; not that we love God, but that He loved us, and sent His Son to be the propitiation for our sins.
THE LAW speaks of what man must do for God.
GRACE tells of what Christ has done for man.
THE LAW addresses man as part of the old creation.

GRACE makes a man a member of the new creation.

THE LAW bears on a nature prone to disobedience.

GRACE creates a nature inclined to obedience.

THE LAW demands obedience by the terror of the Lord.

GRACE beseeches men by the mercies of God.

THE LAW demands holiness.

GRACE gives holiness.

THE LAW says—Condemn him.

GRACE says—Embrace him.

THE LAW speaks of priestly sacrifices offered year by year continually, which could never make the comers thereunto perfect.

GRACE says—But this Man, after he had offered one sacrifice for sins forever . . . by one offering hath perfected forever them that are sanctified.

THE LAW declares—That as many as have sinned in the Law, shall be judged by the Law.

GRACE brings eternal peace to the troubled soul of every child of God, and proclaims God's salvation in defiance of the accusations of the adversary. "He that heareth my word, and believeth on him that sent me, hath everlasting life, and shall not come into condemnation, but is passed from death unto life."

Living Through Giving

We can join the angels in bringing happiness to others

God is the source of life and light and joy to the universe. Like rays of light from the sun, like the streams of water bursting from a living spring, blessings flow out from Him to all His creatures. And wherever the life of God is in the hearts of men, it will flow out to others in love and blessings.

Our Savior's joy was in the uplifting and redemption of fallen men. For this He counted not His life dear unto Himself, but endured the cross, despising the shame. So angels are ever engaged in working for the happiness of others. This is their joy. That which selfish hearts would regard as humiliating service, ministering to those who are wretched and in every way inferior in character and rank, is the work of sinless angles. The spirit of Christ's self-sacrificing love is the spirit that pervades heaven, and is the very essence of its bliss. This is the spirit that Christ's followers will possess, the work that they will do in giving.

When the love of Christ is enshrined in the heart, like sweet fragrance it cannot be hidden. Its holy influence will be felt by all with whom we come in contact. The spirit of Christ in the hearts is like a spring in the desert, flowing to refresh all, and making those who are ready to perish, eager to drink of the water of life.

Love to Jesus will be manifested in a desire to work as He worked, for the blessing and uplifting of humanity. It will lead to love, tenderness, and sympathy toward all the creatures of our heavenly Father's.

The Savior's life on earth was not a life of ease and devotion to Himself, but He toiled with persistent, earnest, untiring effort for the salvation of lost mankind. From the manger to Calvary He followed the path of self-denial, and sought not to be released from arduous tasks, painful travels, and exhausting care and labor. He said, "the Son of Man did not come to be served, but to serve, and to give His life a ransom for many." Matthew 20:28. This was the one great object of His life. Everything else was secondary and subservient. It was His meat and drink to do the will of God and to finish His work. Self and self-interest had no part in His labor.

So those who are the partakers of the grace of Christ will be ready to make any sacrifice, that others for whom He died may share the heavenly gift. They will do all they can to make the world better for their stay in it. This spirit is the sure outgrowth of a soul truly converted. No sooner does one come to Christ, than there is born in his heart a desire to make known to others what a precious friend he has found in Jesus; the saving and sanctifying truth cannot be shut up in his heart. If we are clothed with the righteousness of Christ, and are filled with the joy of His indwelling Spirit, we shall not be able to hold our peace. If we have tasted and seen that the Lord is good, we shall have something to tell. Like Philip when he found the Savior, we shall invite others into His presence. We shall seek to present to them the attractions of Christ, and the unseen realities of the world to come. There will be an intensity of desire to follow in the path that Jesus trod. There will be an earnest longing that those around us may behold "The Lamb of God who takes away the sins of the world!" JOHN 1:29

And the effort to bless others will react in blessings upon ourselves. This was the purpose of God in giving up a part to act in the plan of redemption. He has granted men the privilege of becoming partakers of the divine nature, and, in their turn, of diffusing blessings to their fellow men. This is the highest honor, the greatest joy that it is possible for God to bestow upon men. Those who thus become participants in labors of love are brought nearest to their Creator.

God might have committed the message of the gospel, and all the work of loving ministry, to the heavenly angels. He might have employed other means for accomplishing His purpose. But in His infinite love He chose to make us co-workers with Himself, with Christ and the angels, that we might share the blessings, the joy, the spiritual uplifting, which results from this unselfish ministry.

We are brought into sympathy with Christ through the fellowship of His suffering. Every act of self-sacrifice for the good of others strengthens the spirit of beneficence in the giver's heart, allying him more closely to the Redeemer of the world, who "was rich, yet for your sakes He became poor, that you through His poverty might become rich." II CORINTHIANS 8:9. And it is only as we thus fulfill the divine purpose in our creation, that life can be a blessing to us.

If you will go to work as Christ designs that His disciples shall, and win souls for Him, you will feel the need of a deeper experience and a greater knowledge in divine things, and will hunger and thirst after righteousness. You will plead with God, and your faith will be strengthened, and your soul will drink deeper drafts at the well of salvation. Encountering opposition and trials will drive you to the Bible and to prayer. You will grow in grace and the knowledge of Christ, and will develop a rich experience.

The spirit of unselfish labor for others gives depth, stability, and Christlike loveliness to the character, and brings peace and happiness to its possessor.

The aspirations are elevated. There is no room for sloth or selfishness. Those who thus exercise the Christian graces will grow and will become strong to work for God. They will have clear spiritual perceptions, a steady, growing faith, and an increased power in prayer. The Spirit of God, moving upon their spirit, calls forth the sacred harmonies of the soul, in answer to the divine touch. Those who thus devote themselves to unselfish effort for the good of others, are most surely working out their own salvation.

The only way to grow in grace is to be disinterestedly doing the very work which Christ has enjoined upon us—to engage, to the extent of our ability, in helping and blessing those who need the help we can give them. Strength comes by exercise; activity is the very condition of life. Those who endeavor to maintain Christian life by passively accepting the blessings that come through the means of grace, and doing nothing for Christ, are simply trying to live by eating without working. And in the spiritual as in the natural world, this always results in degeneration and decay. A man who would refuse to exercise his limbs would soon lose all power to use them. Thus the Christian, who will not exercise his God-given powers, not only fails to grow up into Christ, but he loses the strength that he already had.

The church of Christ is God's appointed agency for the salvation of men. Its mission is to carry the gospel to the world. And the obligation rests upon all Christians. Everyone, to the extent of his talent and opportunity, is to fulfill the Savior's commission. The love of Christ, revealed to us, makes us debtors to all who know Him not. God has given us light, not for ourselves alone, but to shed upon them.

If the followers of Christ were awake to duty, there is one today, proclaiming the gospel in heathen lands. And all who could not personally engage in the work, would yet sustain it with their means, their sympathy, and their prayers. And there would be far more earnest labor for souls in Christian countries.

We need not go to heathen lands, or even leave the narrow circle of the home, if it is there that our duty lies, in order to work for Christ. We can do this in the home circle, in the church, among those with whom we associate, and with whom we do business.

The greater part of our Savior's life on earth was spent in patient toil in the carpenter's shop at Nazareth. Ministering angels attended the Lord of life as He walked side by side with peasants and laborers, unrecognized and unhonored. He was as faithfully fulfilling His mission while working at His humble trade as when He healed the sick or walked upon the storm-tossed waves of Galilee. So in the humblest duties and lowliest positions of life, we may walk and work with Jesus.

The apostle says, "Let every man, wherein he is called, therein abide with God." I CORINTHIANS 7:24. The businessman may conduct his business in a way that will glorify his Master because of his fidelity. If he is a true follower of Christ, he will carry his religion into everything that is done, and reveal to men the spirit of Christ. The mechanic may be a diligent and faithful representative of Him who toiled in the lowly walks of life among the hills of Galilee. Everyone who names the name of Christ should so work that others, by seeing his good works, may be led to glorify their Creator and Redeemer.

Many have excused themselves from rendering their gifts to the service of Christ because others were possessed of superior endowments and advantages. The opinion has prevailed that only those who are especially talented are required to consecrate their abilities to the service of God. It has come to be understood by many that talents are given to only a certain favored class, to the exclusion of others, who, of course, are not called upon to share in the toils or the rewards. But it is not so represented in the parable. When the master of the house called his servants, he gave to every man *his* work.

With a loving spirit we may perform life's humblest duties "as to the Lord." COLOSSIANS 3:23. If the love of God is in the heart, it will be manifested in the life. The sweet savor of Christ will surround us, and our influence will elevate and bless.

You are not to wait for great occasions or to expect extraordinary abilities before you go to work for God. You need not have a thought of what the world will think of you. If your daily life is a testimony to the purity and sincerity of your faith, and others are convinced that you desire to benefit them, your efforts will not be wholly lost.

The humblest and poorest of the disciples of Jesus can be a blessing to others. They may not realize that they are doing any special good, but by their unconscious influence they may start waves of blessing that will widen and deepen, and the blessed results they may never know until the day of final reward. They do not feel or know that they are doing anything great. They are not required to weary themselves with anxiety about success. They have only to go forward quietly, doing faithfully the work that God's providence assigns, and their life will not be in vain. Their own souls will be growing more and more into the likeness of Christ; they are workers together with God in this life, and are thus fitting for the higher work and the unshadowed joy of the life to come.

BOOKS BY KOFI QUAYE
Published and Distributed by Heritage/Mysteek Books

CRISIS IN THE FAMILY [HERITAGE/MYSTEEK BOOKS]

This book tells an too common a story: the cross-cultural conflicts most immigrants face virtually everywhere they go. Everyone who has experienced the immigrant life has dealt with the challenge of coping with life in a country where almost everything—language, culture, religion—differs from what they know or were nurtured with. An African family in New York finds itself in the throes of change; some members of the family welcome the change; others resist it. The result is nothing short of a nightmare.

WHEN THE IMMIGRANT'S DREAM TURNS INTO A NIGHTMARE [HERITAGE/MYSTEEK BOOKS]

An up close and personal look at the problems, traumas, tragedies, challenges as well as the rewards of immigration, emigration and migration as told by people who have experienced them. These are the stories you won't read in the newspapers or see on television. The increasing incidence of suicides in Third World immigrant communities in Europe, North America, Australia, etc, unexplained premature deaths, the disappearance of men and women who are never found, the horror stories of immigrants exploited by unscrupulous employers and criminals.

JOJO IN NEW YORK [Macmillan]

A young African arrives in New York with preconceived notions about life in America; he thinks he knows enough from watching television and reading magazines and books. The real deal is a far cry from what he knows. Only his 'mother wit'-common sense—saves him from the danger that stalks him.

MY TROUBLED LIFE: FROM TRINIDAD-TOBAGO TO THE VIRGIN ISLANDS TO AMERICA. By Mervyn Patrick In Collaboration With Kofi Quaye

The saga of a Trinidadian immigrant whose experiences during his travels span the spectrum from hilarious to tragic to mystical.

Books may be ordered from:
HERITAGE/MYSTEEK BOOKS
P.O. BOX 46
Syracuse, NY, 13210
Tel: 315-471-7899
E-mail: info@mysteek.com

The Blue Brothers and Sisters

Left to right—Frank, James, Walter, Alfred, Otis

Left to right—Carolyn, Gloria, Linda, Nardine, Mary, our mother, Inez [seated]